Attention

Deficit

Disorder

A Different Perception

Attention
Deficit
Disorder

A Different Perception

THOM HARTMANN

Newleaf

Newleaf
an imprint of
Gill & Macmillan Ltd
Goldenbridge
Dublin 8
www.gillmacmillan.ie

with associated companies throughout the world
First published by Newleaf 1999
© Copyright 1993, 1997 by Mythical Intelligence, Inc.
0 7171 2865 2

A catalogue record for this book is available
from the British Library.

5   4   3

Dedicated to

Carl and Jean Hartmann

Gottfried Müller, founder of Salem

Joy Kutz, whose work lives on in our hearts

Foreword

Michael Popkin, Ph.D.

Every once in a while someone comes along who takes a body of knowledge and tilts it in such a way that a new view of the information raises up in a flash of hope and encouragement. Thom Hartmann is one of those people, and through this book he has finally put the concept of ADD into a context that we can appreciate.

With as many as 10% of the western world's children suspected of having ADD, I've often wondered how nature could have made such a mistake. Or was it a mistake? Perhaps we were just overdiagnosing—labeling more children as ADD than was warranted. Thom Hartmann's insight into this phenomenon offers a third alternative—one that both reaffirms the wisdom of nature and the value of all human beings.

As the author and director of Active Parenting, I have spent the past dozen years developing programs to help parents. Each of these programs is based on the idea that the purpose of parenting is "to protect and to prepare children to survive and to thrive in the kind of society in which they will live." All of the skills that we teach to parents in Active Parenting, from discipline to communication to encouragement, are designed to instill in children those qualities that will enable them to thrive in a contemporary democratic society. To approach the critical job of parenting without looking at the world in which our children will live—and the

qualities and skills necessary to thrive in that world—
makes as little sense as, well, let's say trying to hunt
wild bear in the middle of a cornfield.

Yet Thom Hartmann has illuminated the fact that
this is exactly the situation that ADD children and
adults find themselves in, namely, hunters in a farming
society. Although tremendously frustrating for the
ADD person, there is nothing innately defective about
the condition—at least as it is reframed in this book. It
is simply a matter of having some of the right skills for
the wrong time.

There is also something very encouraging in how
ADD is presented as a continuum rather than an ei-
ther/or phenomenon. The signs of ADD, which were
clearly presented and consistent with current thinking
as espoused by the American Psychological Association, becomes a mirror in which I suspect many readers will see aspects of themselves. That these signs are
presented as strengths, as well as areas that may need
to be compensated for in a society of Farmers, will not
only offer encouragement and practical solutions to
those who see themselves on the Hunter side of this
continuum, but offer a fascinating insight into the evolution of humankind and society.

*Dr. Michael Popkin, founder and president of Active Parenting
Publishers based in Marietta, Georgia, developed the first
video-based parent education programs in 1983. Since then Dr.
Popkin has authored and produced several programs, as well as
books, on parenting, loss education, and self-esteem education.
Prior to founding Active Parenting Publishers, Dr. Popkin was
a family therapist practicing in the Atlanta area. Dr. Popkin can
be reached at Active Parenting Publishers, 810 Franklin Court,
Suite B, Marietta, GA 30067.*

Author's Preface

From Minimal Brain Damage to Hyperactivity to ADD

Every noble work is at first impossible.

—Thomas Carlyle

In the spring of 1980, I sat in the living room of the apartment of Dr. Ben Feingold, overlooking the Golden Gate Bridge in San Francisco, listening to him describe his search for a solution to the problem of hyperactivity. At the time, I was Executive Director of a residential treatment facility for abused and abandoned children, and most of the children referred to us had been diagnosed with "hyperactivity" or "minimal brain damage" (or MBD, a term later softened to "minimal brain dysfunction"). I was acutely interested in what Dr. Feingold had to say.

As a pediatric allergist, Dr. Feingold had noticed over the years that a number of his patients with skin disorders (particularly psoriasis) had identifiable allergies. When certain foods or food additives were removed from a child's diet, particularly those containing salicylates (the aspirin-like compounds contained in some foods and many food-additives), sores and crusty skin patches vanished.

But there was an odd side effect to these skin-disease cures: the children's behavior also changed. Many of Dr. Feingold's young patients, in addition to being victims of skin diseases, had been diagnosed with hyperactivity or minimal brain dysfunction. But when the skin-disease-causing foods or food additives were removed from their diets, the hyperactivity quite often disappeared, or was reduced so dramatically that parents and teachers noticed the change.

On the basis of these findings, Dr. Feingold built his theory that minimal brain dysfunction or hyperactivity results from a food or food-additive allergy. His first book, *Why Your Child Is Hyperactive* (Random House, 1975), eventually sparked a nationwide movement. "Feingold parents" set up "Feingold groups," to discuss ways to keep children away from salicylate-containing foods and food-additives. Papers were published, both condemning and supporting Feingold, and across the nation thousands of parents reported dramatic changes with his dietary program.

We tried the Feingold diet at the institution I headed, with excellent results on several children. This early institutional trial became the basis for a report on National Public Radio's *All Things Considered* program and dozens of newspaper and magazine articles. I published an article about our results in *The Journal of Orthomolecular Psychiatry*.

But there were some children with hyperactivity or minimal brain dysfunction—perhaps a majority—

whom the Feingold diet did not help. This troubling inconsistency led many professionals to discard Feingold's hypotheses in whole, and the movement that bears his name is now, several years after his death, just a shell of what it once was.

Yet Dr. Ben Feingold was a pioneer. In the opinion of many people, he discovered a key to one facet of what was later recognized to be not just one disease (the minimal brain dysfunction or hyperactive syndrome), but part of an entire spectrum of behavior disorders, including attention deficit disorder, hyperkinesis, and learning disorders such as dyslexia.

Since Feingold's time, psychiatry has largely separated hyperactivity from ADD. They are now seen as two separate (although sometimes overlapping) things.

Hyperactivity involves restless or excessive (hyper) activity. Hyperactive children are often described as being "on fire," as if they have "ants in their pants." Feingold noted these descriptions, and observed that they were probably having the normal reaction to an allergy—an itch—in the brain.

Attention deficit disorder, on the other hand, may occur without any presence of a hyperactive state. ADD is more clearly described as a person's difficulty focusing on a single thing for any significant period of time. Such people are described as excessively distractible, impatient, impulsive, and often seeking immediate gratification. They often disregard the long-term consequences of their actions, so focused are they on the moment and its rewards. They're usually disorganized and messy, because they bounce from project to project, too impatient to clean up the debris from their last activity (be it making their beds or organizing their desks). But, while ADD children usually have problems with schoolwork, they're not bouncing off the walls like their hyperactive peers.

A third category, "attention deficit hyperactive disorder" (ADHD) represents those who have both ADD and hyperactivity. This includes the majority of hyperactive children, although not all, and was the first category to be recognized in medicine more than seventy-five years ago.

While Ben Feingold believed he had found a "cure" for hyperactivity, he was baffled by his diet's failure to cure children of short attention spans. The hyperactive kids he treated no longer needed restraint or drugs, and a few became quite "normal" on his diet, but many still showed signs of the ADD syndrome which did not respond to diet.

Initially, he'd concluded that children who didn't respond had food allergies not yet discovered (such as an allergy to milk or wheat which are nearly impossible to avoid), or that his subjects were "cheating" on the diet. But a few months before he died, Dr. Feingold shared with me his concerns about this apparent inconsistency in the theory. He wondered out loud if there might be several different disorders lumped into what he had seen as a single category.

Feingold, again a prophet, was right. ADD is now increasingly being recognized as a separate syndrome from hyperactivity, something that is not generally "cured" by dietary change, other than the modest improvements which may result from using sugar in moderation.

It is interesting to note, however, that ADD children and adults often report an inordinate craving for sugar and, occasionally, exhibit some symptoms of hypoglycemia. They may also be more sensitive to the highs and crashes that come from sugar, alcohol, caffeine, and illicit drug consumption (and may benefit from avoiding those substances). But as we will see in a later chapter, these sensitivities may have little or nothing to do with symptoms of a "disease." It is quite probable that they are, instead, indicative of a biochemistry ideally suited to certain fundamental tasks.

Acknowledgments

For the preparation of this manuscript thanks go to those many ADD adults who shared their life stories so others could learn from their successes and failures.

Dianne Breen, who helped give birth to this book, and Dirk E. Huttenbach, MD, an expert in the field of child and adult ADD, were invaluable in providing anecdotes, information, and some of the core concepts which shaped the ideas presented here. G.W. Hall and Carla Nelson did a marvelous job of editing the early manuscript, and Fran and all the folks on CompuServe were a big help.

I owe a special acknowledgement to Dave deBronkart, who liberally shared his knowledge and experience with ADD, and proofread this book so thoroughly that it would not be inaccurate to say that he wrote parts of it. On the subject of ADD, Dave is the most knowledgeable layman I've met, as well as an articulate public speaker and outspoken defender of this world's ADD/Hunters.

Special thanks go to Susan Barrows, one of the world's great proofreaders, who caught at least a hundred typos in the early draft of this book while simultaneously offering valuable editorial assistance, and new and important insights into ADD.

Thanks also to Kyle Roderick and Alexis Fischer

for useful suggestions which added to the content of this book.

An excellent resource for parents of ADD children is the non-profit organization CH.A.D.D., which has chapters nationwide. For the address of a local chapter near you, write to CH.A.D.D., 499 N.W. 70th Ave., Suite 308, Plantation, FL 33317. For educational resources on ADD to individuals and support organizations, write to Attention Deficit Disorder Association (ADDA), PO Box 972, Mentor, OH 44061.

And special thanks are due to my wife, Louise, whose patience and support have helped bring this work (and so many other projects) to fruition.

Some of the money you paid for this book will go to benefit the work of the international Salem projects. For more information about Salem, write to: The Salem International Foundation, Star Route Box 60C, Frostburg, MD 21532; The New England Salem Children's Village, Stinson Lake Rd., Rumney, NH 03266; or: Kinder-und Jugendhilfswerk Salem, 95346 Stadtsteinach, Germany.

Contents

Introduction

—

Edward M. Hallowell, M.D.

Thom Hartmann is a businessman who is also a philosopher, world traveler, spiritualist, hiker, trainer of soldiers, author, lecturer, husband, father, son, and all-around lively human being. He is a twentieth-century pioneer, an adventurer, or as he would say, a hunter.

His idea of the hunter in the farmer's world, which he develops in this newly re-issued book, is just one of his many innovative ideas. This idea came to him when he was reading in bed one day. Never a quiet moment in the Hartmann brain. It is a fascinating idea, one that people from many different walks of life have found extremely helpful in learning how to fit best into today's world.

I won't sound-byte the idea here, but rather report what I have heard from many people around the country, that they have found this idea, as well as Thom's other books and lectures, practical and right on the mark. People mention Thom's name, and their energy level starts to rise.

What Thom offers is help, hope, and heart, as well as considerable thought and life experience. I commend both him and his books to all readers.

Edward Hallowell, M.D., is in private practice in adult and child psychiatry. He is the co-author with John J. Ratey, M.D., of Driven to Distraction and Answers to Distraction.

Author's Introduction

Hunters and Farmers
Five Years Later

There must be no barriers to freedom of inquiry. There is no place for dogma in science. The scientist is free, and must be free to ask any question, to doubt any assertion, to seek for any evidence, to correct any errors.

—J. Robert Oppenheimer, (*Life*, October 10, 1949)

In the five years since the first publication of this book and my presentation of the Hunter/Farmer concept as a possible explanation for why we have ADD in our gene pool, there have been many changes in the thinking of people who study the subject. There have also been many changes in the overall view of psychiatric and physiological disorders in general, particularly those with a genetic basis.

The publication of *Why We Get Sick: The New Science of Darwinian Medicine* by Randolph Nesse M.D. and George Williams Ph.D. (Times Books) signaled a turning point in the minds of many. The book, thoroughly researched and brilliantly well-written, makes the strong and scientifically-defendable case that we are creatures living out of our element, humans with bodies and brains designed to live in a primitive natural environment and still carrying around the physical and psychological tools necessary to that environment. These include things from morning sickness to cystic fibrosis to depression. Our modern lifestyle, evolved just over the past few thousand years, represents not a norm for human life, but an incredibly brief flicker of momentary history in the 200,000 year life-span of *Homo sapiens* (people like us) on the planet.

Robert Wright's book *The Moral Animal* carries the model a step further, dealing with the subject of "Darwinian psychology," and pointing out in dramatic detail how behaviors ranging from depression to aggression to infidelity were adaptive and useful in the very-recent history of the human race.

The March 27, 1995 issue of *Time* featured a cover story on the functions of the brain and the latest research into why our brains behave the way the way they do. Evolutionary notions of behavior played an important part in that article, including the recent discovery by researchers that those people most likely to have the gene that causes the brain to crave fatty foods and thus produce obesity are also those people whose ancestors over the past 10,000 years came from parts of the world where famines were common. What was an adaptive behavior for primitive peoples has become maladaptive in a world where most "hunting" is done at the supermarket.

The 1996 publication by psychiatrists and physicians Anthony Stevens and John Price of the book

Evolutionary Psychiatry: a New Beginning (Routledge) summarized much of this research, and has provided a deep mine of material for future researchers. For example, they tell the story of the Ik, a group of hunter-gatherer peoples in Uganda whose rates of life-threatening psychological and physical illnesses exploded when they were forcibly moved from their natural hunting grounds and forced to engage in agriculture. Other examples abound in this well-researched work.

WHERE HAVE ALL THE HUNTERS GONE?

Additionally, new advances in anthropology and paleontology have answered one of the most vexing questions about the Hunter/Farmer theory: *"Why is the leftover Hunter/ADD gene only present in a minority of our population, and where have all the hunters gone?"*

In popular literature, Riane Eisler (*The Chalice and the Blade* and *Sacred Pleasures*) has explored early cultures and shows the fundamental differences between what she calls "cooperator" and "dominator" cultures. (We in western civilization are members of the latter.) Similarly, Daniel Quinn (*Ishmael* and *The Story of B*) writes about "Leavers" and "Takers" to describe a similar cultural division. About five thousand years ago, these cultural schisms set the stage for a mass extermination of hunter/gatherer peoples which continues to this day in remote parts of Africa, Asia, and the Americas.

A brilliant study published in the February, 1994 issue of *Discover* magazine detailed the exact answer to the question of when and how this happened, and has since been corroborated by other researchers. Using an analysis of language patterns and DNA, researchers found that 3,000 years ago Africa was almost entirely populated by thousands of different (genetically and in language) tribes of hunter/gatherer peoples. Population density was low and, apparently, strife was minimal.

Then a group of Bantu-speaking agriculturists in the northwestern part of Africa were apparently infected with what University of California professor of Native American Studies Jack Forbes calls the "cultural mental illness" of *Wétiko* (a native American term for the amoral and predatory behavior of the European invaders). *Wétiko* is the term that Forbes applied decades ago to describe what Eisler and Quinn today call "dominator" and "taker" cultural mass psychology.

In his penetrating and thought-provoking book *Columbus and Other Cannibals*, Professor Forbes points out how *Wétiko*, which he calls a "highly-contagious form of mental illness," originated in Mesopotamia around 5,000 years ago. From there, it spread across the fertile crescent and into Syria, eventually infecting northern Africa, Europe (via the Roman conquerors who carried Wétiko), Asia, and, with the arrival of Columbus, the Americas.

The Bantu-speaking farmers of northwest Africa, culturally contaminated by *Wétiko* beliefs in the "correctness" of genocide, systematically spread across the entire African continent over a 2,000-year period, destroying every group in their path. The result is that now fewer than one percent of the entire African continent's population are hunter/gatherers, and the languages and cultures of thousands of tribes—developed over 200,000 years of human history—have been lost forever. Entire ethnic groups were wiped out and have now vanished from the Earth.

The reasons the *Wétiko* farmers were so successful in their conquest of Africa (and later, Europe, Asia, Australia, and the Americas) is fourfold:

1. Farming is more efficient than hunting at producing food. Because it's about ten times more efficient at extracting calories from the soil, the population density of farming communities tend to be about ten times higher than those of hunting communities. And so their armies were ten times larger.

2. Farmers become immune to the diseases of their own animals. Measles, chicken pox, mumps, influenza and numerous other diseases originated in—and are still often carried by—domesticated animals. When the farmers of Europe first came to the shores of the Americas, they killed off millions of native Americans through accidental infection with these diseases, to which the local hunters had not developed immunities. (This later escalated with the deliberate infection of entire tribes with smallpox-infected blankets by the *Wétiko*-infected invaders.)

3. Farming is stable. Farmers tend to stay in one place, and that gives rise to specialization of function. The butcher, baker, candlestick maker, and weapons maker came into being, and armies were formed. Factories were a logical extension of farming technologies, and so farming peoples became even more efficient at producing weapons and technologies of destruction.

4. The *Wétiko* culture taught that slaughter could be justified on religious grounds. From its beginnings in Mesopotamia, *Wétiko* taught that the slaughter of other humans was not only acceptable, but could even be "a good thing" because it was ordered or sanctioned by their gods. The most bizarre instance of this can be seen during the Crusades, when Europeans slaughtered "heathens" in order to "save their souls." A close second is "the winning of the American West," in which Americans (whose Declaration of Independence says the Creator gave people the right to life, liberty and the pursuit of happiness) decreed that the same Creator gave white Europeans a "Manifest Destiny" to overtake the whole continent, and used this religious argument to justify killing the "heathen" residents.

While indigenous hunting peoples often had conflict with neighbors over borders and territories, these conflicts served to strengthen the cultural and independent identities of both tribes involved. *Wétiko* warfare, where every last person in the "competing" tribe is put to death, is something that no anthropologist has ever found in the history or behavior of any past or modern non-*Wétiko* hunting/gathering peoples. The *Wétiko* agriculturists, however, viewing non-Wétiko humans to be as exploitable as the land, have a history littered with genocide, slavery, and exploitation.

And so, over the past 5000 years, on every continent and among every people, hunter/gatherers have been wiped out, displaced, slaughtered, exterminated, and oppressed by *Wétiko* farmers/industrialists. Today, fewer than 2% of the world's human population are genetically pure hunter/gatherer peoples, and only a remnant of them is found in our gene pool, and that only as the result of enslavement and assimilation.

THOSE WHO WOULD DISEMPOWER FOR THEIR OWN GAIN

The *Wétiko* domination continues in our modern world.

We live in a society so psychologically sick that Mafia kingpins who sell dope and prostitution and order the murder of others live in expensive houses in "nice" neighborhoods. We honor those who have "attained success," even if they do it by selling death-dealing substances like tobacco. "Dog eat dog" is a cliché and norm in our culture, and the idea of cooperating instead of dominating is considered quaint and "nice" but idealistic and ineffective. It's assumed that to be successful in business one must lie and cheat, and our political leaders are trusted by such a pitiful minority of citizens (fewer than 20% in recent polls) that it's doubtful our governments could continue to operate if they didn't control the police, the prisons, and the tax apparatus (which is enforced by the police and prisons).

In the middle of this cultural milieu, we find those of the "helping professions." The majority enter these fields because of an honest and sincere desire to be of service to others. Much good is done and many lives are improved and even saved, and we rightfully have afforded these people a place of honor in our society. Yet within and on the fringes of these professions are also exploiters who proffer dubious advice or outright quack technologies. These controversial treatments range from injecting children with radioactive substances prior to "scanning" their brains, to hugely-marked-up herbal supplements accompanied by inflated claims, to expensive and prolonged (often for years) brand-name "therapies."

Essential to the success of the exploiters is the concept of sickness.

It is well known in the business world that if you can convince people something is wrong with them, you can then make a lot of money selling them a remedy. It's been done with facial hair, body odor, leg hair, wrinkles, varicose veins, "bad" breath, and dozens of what used to be ordinary parts of the human condition. Convince people there's something wrong with or embarrassing about their normal functions and you can get rich selling them mouthwash, douches, depilatory creams, wrinkle removers, suntan aids, diet pills, and a host of other products.

Similarly, exploiters on the fringes of the medical arena depend on the notion of sickness or abnormality to peddle their wares: to sell, they depend on convincing you that there's something about you that's intolerable, something that is wrong, something you need to change. In this context we hear some speakers and authors talk about the "importance of taking seriously" ADD.

Their message is not, "If you feel you have a problem, I have some solutions that may work," but, rather, "You are sick and I am not, and you must unquestioningly let me help you with my cure."

If we agree there is a need but we question the treatment, *our* intentions are challenged: "Why are you questioning me when I'm only trying to help you and your child?"

I will be among the first to say that being a Hunter in this Farmer's world is fraught with difficulty: nobody can deny that. The failures, evident in our prisons and schools and street people, offer loud testimony to the seriousness of ADD in today's society.

But to say, "Everything is okay with our culture and society, so it must be *you* that's seriously screwed up and needs treatment," is totally disempowering. It robs people of their humanity and dignity. It subjugates them. It is *Wétiko*.

I much prefer a rational middle ground, well articulated by Harvard Medical School associate professor of psychiatry Dr. John Ratey in his foreword to my 1995 book *ADD Success Stories*:

> After Thom Hartmann's first two books on ADD, the metaphor of the hunter began to provide many ADDers with an acceptable label for their quirkiness and a way of looking at themselves that was full of hope and permission.

> Just as the diagnosis of ADD itself often helps in replacing guilt with hope, so does an appealing metaphor like that of a hunter (which smacks of Robin Hood and Madame Curie) help in giving many people a sense of purpose and direction.

> This sort of personal mythology can provide a platform that looks to the future with promise and approval—never masking the problems of the ADD brain but instead offering role models to guide the ADDer into a more optimistic and forward-looking journey.

> While this new reframed version of who they are should never excuse foibles or open the door to self-indulgence, being granted permission to be who they are often drives individuals to reach previously unattempted heights. When the shackles of shame are lifted, the future can be approached with a cleaner, crisper, more energetic viewpoint.

WHERE DO WE GO FROM HERE?

And so, five years after the first publication of this book, we are left with the ongoing questions: *What is ADD, where did it come from, why do we have it, and where do we go from here?*

While scientists do not yet know for sure what the mechanism or cause of ADD is, we *do* know from numerous studies that when we describe and define people, they will most often live up to that expectation.

Tell a child he's "bad" often enough, and he'll most likely become bad. Tell her she's "brilliant," and she'll strive to achieve brilliance.

Not only do we live up to the things others tell us out loud about ourselves, we also live up to the unspoken assumptions.

The most famous example of this is the study in which a group of elementary school students were divided into two groups, balanced as much as possible by the researchers to be identical in the average of their abilities and intelligence. Then the teachers were told that group A was the highly intelligent group, and that group B was the lower intelligence group.

By the end of a single semester, group A had significantly outperformed group B academically. This wasn't just the grade the teacher gave them; it was *their actual performance* on a standardized test. Their real-life performance was substantially affected by what the teacher expected of them—even when the teacher didn't realize it.

Children *can* find and achieve their best when the adults around them help them do so.

Particularly as children, we respond to other's expectations of us. We live up to their assumptions, and we perform up to their and our belief of our ability to perform.

While there has never, ever been a study positively correlating grades in school with psychological success or adjustment in later life, there have been many which show that childhood self-esteem is a significant and generally accurate predictor of adult competence. (The book *Emotional Intelligence* by Daniel Goleman contains a wealth of this research.)

So when my son, at age 13, was diagnosed with ADD and was told that he had a "disease" that is "similar to diabetes, but instead of your pancreas being damaged and not producing enough insulin, your brain has been damaged and isn't producing enough neurotransmitters," I knew in my gut it was a lousy, disempowering story.

Not only was the message, "You're broken and we're the only ones who can fix you," but there was also an implicit, "You're broken and can never be *really* normal." In my opinion, that message profanes the sacred reality of human life and human diversity by putting people in neat little categories (which, it turns out, aren't so neat) and by then telling them that their future can only be good if they follow the dictates of the person who has redefined them.

This is well illustrated by a short semi-autobiographical story by Joe Parsons, a writer I met on the Internet. I reprint it here with his permission:

> "Dad! Dad! Look at my report card!" I let the screen door slam behind me and stood in front of my father, clutching my now-wrinkled report card.
>
> "What do you have there, Dave Jr.? Report card? Let me see it." He glanced at my grades—two C's, a D, and an A-minus. He looked down at me, frowning.
>
> "Didja see the comments, Dad? Didja? I brought that F in math up to a D! I'm gonna pass it! And look at what my teachers said, Dad!" I had read my report card over and over as I ran home. Three of my teachers said I was making "good progress" and my English teacher said, "Dave Jr. has a refreshing and creative point of view." My father kept looking at my report card, then at me. He didn't say anything for a long time.
>
> Finally, he said, "Son, these grades just aren't very good, but I know you're doing the best you

can." He sat me down on the sofa and looked at me. He seemed to be real sad. "Let me explain it to you again, son; you know those pills I have to make you take?"

"Yeah, Dad, the Ritalin... so I can pay attention better in class; they're really helping."

He looked even sadder. "Yes, son. It's a very strong medicine we have to give you because you have this very serious disease called Attention-Deficit-Disorder.'" He said it slowly, to make sure I would understand. "You see, you're not like the other kids. There's something wrong with your brain that makes you different from the other... normal... kids. When the teacher says that you have a..." he looked at the report card again. "...'refreshing and creative point of view,' what she's really saying is that you can't fit in and say things the way the other kids do."

"Is that a bad thing, Dad?"

He put his hand on my head. "I'm afraid it is, Son, but we're just going to have to live with your being ... different."

"But my teacher said I was doing a lot better, Dad; she said I was creative! Isn't that a good thing, Dad?"

He smiled at me again, but he still looked sad. "Your teacher is just trying to make you feel better, son. She doesn't realize that your disease is going to make you mess up everything you do in your life. The sooner you realize that, the easier it will be for you. I just don't want you to be disappointed, son."

I started to feel sad, too. I looked down at my father's shoes. "What am I going to do, Dad?"

"Just do the best you can, son. The main thing is not to get your hopes up." He put his arm around my shoulders. "As long as you always realize that you're different from the normal people that aren't sick like you are, you'll be a lot happier."

"Okay, Dad. I'll try to remember." I took the report card from him and went to my room. I sat on my bed and read the words over and over: "good progress...refreshing and creative point of view."

Soon tears blurred the words and I tossed the card on the floor. I knew Dad was right: I would always mess up.

I was glad he reminded me.

I know this father meant well; he was doing the best he knew how, to respond to what he'd been told about his son's situation.

Unlike the father in this story, I spent the first year after my son's diagnosis (and the sermon by his psychologist that he isn't "normal") trying to find a deeper understanding of what this thing called ADD was. I read everything I could find, and talked with friends and former associates in the child-care industry. I learned that the three cardinal indicators of ADD are *distractibility, impulsiveness,* and *a love of high stimulation or risk.* (If you toss in the inability to sit still—hyperactivity—you have ADD-H or ADHD.) While I'd never seen it written anywhere, I also intuitively knew that people with ADD had a different sense of time from those without ADD.

And the more I looked at it, the more it seemed that this "illness" could also be an asset under some circumstances.

After six months of hyperfocused research, I was reading myself to sleep one night with *Scientific American.* The article was about how the end of the ice age, 12,000 years ago, brought about a mutation of grasses leading to the first appearance on earth of what we today call wheat and rice. These early cereal grains led to the development of agriculture among humans, and that point in history is referred to as the Agricultural Revolution.

As the article went into greater detail about how the agricultural revolution transformed human society, I got a "Eureka!" that was such a jolt I sat straight up in bed. "People with ADD are the descendants of hunters!" I said to my wife Louise, who gave me a baffled look. "They'd have to be constantly scanning their environment, looking for food and for threats to them: that's distractibility. They'd have to make instant decisions and act on them without a second's thought when they're chasing or being chased through the forest or jungle, which is impulsivity. And they'd have to love the high-stimulation and risk-filled environment of the hunting field."

"What are you talking about?" she said.

"ADD!" I said, waving my hands. "It's only a flaw if you're in a society of farmers!"

From that concept came what was originally a metaphor, an empowering story that I could tell my son (for whom I originally wrote this book) and others to explain their "difference" in a positive light. Since that time, we've discovered that this "story" may in fact be factually accurate: science is rapidly corroborating many of those original observations and theories.

So where we go from here is forward, into a future where people with ADD are not embarrassed or ashamed to say they are different, where children are helped in schools with appropriate interventions and tailored educational environments, and where teenagers and adults recognize in advance that some jobs or careers or mates are well-suited to their temperament and others are not. From that self-knowledge all ADDers can gain a greater measure of success in life.

We go forward as Hunters.

Northfield, VT
June, 1997

Chapter One

—

ADD as a State of Mind

*Know the true value of time. Snatch, seize, and
enjoy every moment of it. No idleness, no laziness, no
procrastination. Never put off 'til tomorrow what you
can do today.* —Lord Chesterfield

Somewhere between six and twenty million men,
women, and children in the United States have attention deficit disorder or ADD. Millions more individuals
possess many ADD-type characteristics even though
they may have learned to cope so well that they don't
think of themselves as people with attention-related
problems.

If you are an adult who has experienced chronic
issues with restlessness, impatience, poor listening
skills, or a difficulty doing "boring" jobs like balancing
a checkbook, you already know what it feels like to
experience some of the challenges associated with
ADD. And if you're the parent of an ADD child, the
chances are high you have at least some ADD traits
yourself.

This book is the first I know of to present the idea

1

that ADD is not always a disorder—but instead may be a trait of personality and metabolism; that ADD comes from a specific evolutionary need in the history of humankind; that ADD can actually be an advantage (depending on circumstances); and that, through an understanding of the mechanism which led to ADD's presence in our gene pool, we can recreate our schools and workplaces to not only accommodate ADD individuals, but to allow them to again become the powers behind cultural, political, and scientific change which they have so often historically represented.

You will see that this state of mind evolved naturally. It's not at all a malfunction—to the contrary, it's a coherent, functioning response to a different kind of world and society than that in which many of us live.

If, as you read this book, you see yourself described, it may hit you as a revelation. I've shared this information with many ADD adults, and invariably they are startled, concerned, and ultimately pleased to finally understand one of the principal forces which have shaped their lives.

This knowledge frees them to reframe the way they view their jobs, their relationships, their frustrations—which are usually legion—and their goals. It helps them set new courses and directions which may lead to greater success in life than they ever dreamed possible, or directs them to therapy or medication that will help them adjust to life in a non-ADD world and workplace.

If you're the father or mother of an ADD child, odds are high that you're an ADD adult yourself, to some extent. While long viewed as a condition that mostly affects young boys (the diagnosed prevalence in children is around 7:1, male-to-female), some authorities find that the rate of ADD among adults is 1:1, male-to-female. This gender differential may be skewed by many factors, including the fact that adult women are more likely to seek psychiatric care and therefore have a higher rate of diagnosis later in life. On the other hand, boys in our culture are, according to some studies, trained to be more aggressive and outspoken than girls. Combine this with ADD, and we may have a situation where ADD boys stand out more visibly than ADD girls, and therefore, at least in childhood, are more likely to be diagnosed.

This book does not advocate the abandonment of traditional diagnostic or treatment tools, including drugs such as Ritalin and behavioral modification therapy, for ADD. Indeed, you will see a strong case made for the proposition that such tools are often the salvation of people with ADD.

It is my hope that this book will help us remove the stigma of "illness" or "deficit" associated with a diagnosis of ADD and related conditions. A second, and equally important, goal is to provide specific tools to "work around" the dilemma of being an ADD "Hunter" in a contemporary society which is largely structured for and by non-ADD "Farmers," a concept we will explore in detail.

The individuals with whom I've shared this theory have found it both positive and transformational. This is the spirit in which this book is offered, with the sincere hope that it may help more teachers, psychologists, psychiatrists, and parents to empower and enable rather than label as sick or disabled ADD children and adults.

Chapter Two

━━

How to Recognize Attention Deficit Disorder

Genius all over the world stands hand in hand, and one shock of recognition runs the whole circle round.
—Herman Melville (Hawthorne and His Mosses, 1850)

ADD is not an all-or-nothing diagnosis. There appears to be a curve of behaviors and personality types, ranging from extremely-non-ADD to extremely-ADD. Although there has not yet been enough research in the field to know the shape of this curve, it probably resembles a bell curve, with the majority of "normal" individuals falling somewhere in the center, showing a few ADD-like characteristics, and a minority (perhaps somewhere around 20-30 percent of the population) being split up on the two extreme ends of the spectrum.

Since a large body of research indicates that ADD is a hereditary condition, the distribution of this curve may well reflect the intermixing over the years of the genetic material of ADD and non-ADD individuals, blurring the edges of both types of behaviors. Placed along the spectrum of ADD individuals you will find people who typically exhibit some or all of the following characteristics:

❖ **Easily distracted.** ADD people are constantly monitoring the scene; they notice everything that's going on, and particularly notice changes or quickly changing things in their environment. (This is the reason why, for example, it's difficult to have a conversation with ADD people when a television is on in the room; their attention will constantly wander back to the television and its rapidly-changing inputs.)

❖ **Short, but extraordinarily intense, attention span.** Oddly enough, this isn't definable in terms of minutes or hours: some tasks will bore an ADD person in thirty seconds, other projects may hold their rapt attention for hours, days, or even months. ADD adults often have difficulty holding a job for an extended period of time, not because they're incompetent but because they become "bored." Similarly, ADD adults often report multiple marriages, or "extremely intense, but short" relationships. When tested for attention span on a boring, uninteresting task, ADD people tend to score significantly lower than others.

❖ **Disorganization, accompanied by snap decisions.** ADD children and adults are often chronically disorganized. Their rooms are a shambles, their desks are messy, their files are incoherent; their living or working areas look like a bomb went off. This is also a common characteristic of non-ADD people, possibly related to upbringing or culture, but something usually separates messy ADD folks from their non-ADD counterparts: non-ADD people can usually find what they need in their messes, while ADD people typically can't find anything. An ADD person may be working on a project when something else distracts him, and he makes the snap decision to change priorities and jump into the new project- leaving behind the debris from the previous project. One ADD adult commented that "the great thing about being disorganized is that I'm constantly making exciting discoveries. Sometimes I'll find things I didn't even know I'd lost!"

❖ **Distortions of time-sense.** Most non-ADD people describe time as a fairly consistent and linear flow. ADD individuals, on the other hand, have an exaggerated sense of urgency when they're on a task, and an exaggerated sense of boredom when they feel they have nothing to do. This sense of boredom often leads to the abuse of substances such as alcohol and drugs, which alter the perception of time, whereas the sense of fast-time when on a project leads to chronic impatience. This elastic sense of time also causes many ADD adults to describe emotional highs and lows as having a profound impact on them. The lows, particularly, may seem as if they'll last forever, whereas the highs are often perceived as flashing by.

❖ **Difficulty following directions.** This has traditionally been considered a subset of the ADD person's characteristic of not being able to focus on something they consider boring, meaningless, or unimportant. While receiving directions, conventional wisdom has it that ADD people are often monitoring their environment as well, noticing other things, thinking of other things, and, in general, not paying attention. In other words, ADD people frequently have difficulty following directions, because the directions weren't fully received and understood in the first place.

Another theory to explain this is that ADD people are very independent, and tend to dislike being told what to do. They prefer to think for themselves, and may therefore place less importance on other's directions.

But the most likely explanation for this, according to some authorities in the field, is that people with ADD have difficulty processing auditory or verbal information.

When you say to a "normal" person "Go to the store and pick up a bottle of milk, a loaf of bread, and some orange juice, then stop at the gas station and fill up the car on the way home," the "normal" person will create a mental picture of each of those things as they hear them described. They picture the store, the milk, the bread, the juice, and the gas station. This congruence of verbal and visual images makes for high-quality memory.

But an ADD person may only hear the words- without creating the mental pictures so vital to memory. They drive off to the store, repeating to themselves, "Milk, bread, juice, gas; milk, bread, juice, gas ..." until something distracts them and they lose the entire memory.

This problem with auditory processing is fairly well documented among children with ADD. However, the percentage of its prevalence among the general, non-ADD population is unknown. It may be that ADD people are only slightly more likely to have this problem, or it may be a cardinal symptom/problem.

One ADD adult described it this way: "I find my comprehension of long chains of words is improved, vastly, by a picture. That way my brain can directly absorb the pattern. If you un-pattern it and translate it into a linear string of words, then I'm forced to absorb the string and reconstruct the pattern."

This may also account for the so-very-common reports from parents of ADD children that their kids are television addicts and hate to read. Reading requires the processing of auditory information (words sounded out within the brain into internal pictures), whereas television is purely external visualization. At the residential treatment facility I ran in New Hampshire, we found it useful to remove the televisions altogether from the residences of ADD children. After a few months, the kids began reading, and the habit persisted after the reintroduction of television.

There's also a debate about the cause of the ADD/auditory processing problem.

One camp says that it's the result of a hard-wiring problem in the brain—the same mis-wiring problem that causes other ADD symptoms.

The other camp theorizes that converting auditory information to visual information is a learned behavior, acquired by most people about the time they become proficient with language, between ages two and five. Because ADD people "weren't paying attention," they may be more likely to have simply missed out on learning this vital skill.

Since the skill of converting words to pictures can be taught to ADD people with relative ease, the latter theory appears probable. Just say to an ADD child, "Will you please visualize that?" and watch for the characteristic movement of their eyes toward the ceiling, which usually means they're creating an internal mental image. If this is done each time instructions are given to an ADD child, eventually (often in a matter of weeks) the child will learn this basic skill of auditory processing and it becomes second nature. (For ADD adults, Harry Lorayne's Memory Book is wonderful, with its heavy emphasis on several methods to teach this skill, along with what Lorayne calls original awareness, which is merely a painless method of teaching yourself to pay attention.)

❖ **Exhibit occasional symptoms of depression**, or daydream more than others. ADD individuals who are relatively self-aware about the issues of sugar and food metabolism often report that depression or tiredness follows a meal or the consumption of sugary foods. This reaction may be related to differences in glucose (sugar) metabolism between ADD and non-ADD people, which we'll discuss in more detail later.

Another possibility is that ADD people are simply bored more often by the lack of challenges presented by our schools, jobs, and culture, and this boredom translates for some people into depression.

❖ **Take risks.** ADD individuals seem to have strong swings of emotion and conviction, and make faster decisions than non-ADD types. While this trait often leads to disaster (I've spoken with several psychiatrists who suggest that, in their experience, American prison populations may be up to 90 percent ADD), it also means that ADD individuals are frequently the spark plugs of our society, the shakers and movers, the people who bring about revolution and change. ADD expert Dr. Edna Copeland, in a 1992 Atlanta speech, referenced a recent study which indicates that about half of all entrepreneurs test out as being ADD.

Evidence is strong that many of our Founding Fathers were also ADD (see the chapter titled *Hunters Who Have Changed the World*). If they hadn't been, the United States of America might never have come into being. ADD risk-takers may have predominated in the early Americas because those were the people best suited to undertake the voyage to this continent and face the unknown.

❖ **Easily frustrated and impatient.** To "not suffer fools gladly" is a classic ADD characteristic. While others may beat around the bush, searching for diplomacy, an ADD individual is most often direct, to the point, and can't understand how or why such bluntness might give offense. And when things aren't working out, "Do Something!" becomes the ADD person's rallying cry- even if the something is sloppy or mistaken.

WHAT THE EXPERTS SAY

The American Psychiatric Association's DSM III-R defined a person as having attention deficit hyperactive disorder (ADHD) if they meet eight or more of the criteria paraphrased here. As of this writing, this is the only "official" method for diagnosing ADHD, in children or adults:

1. When required to remain seated, a person has difficulty doing so.
2. Stimuli extraneous to the task at hand are easily distracting.
3. Holding attention to a single task or play activity is difficult.
4. Frequently will hop from one activity to another, without completing the first.
5. Fidgets or squirms (or feels restless mentally).
6. Doesn't want to, or can't, wait for his or her turn when involved in group activities.
7. Before a question is completely asked, will often interrupt the questioner with an answer.
8. Has problems with job or chore follow-through, and this difficulty doesn't stem from some other learning disability or defiant behavior.
9. Can't play quietly without difficulty.
10. Impulsively jumps into physically dangerous ac-

tivities without weighing the consequences. (This is different from garden-variety thrill-seeking, and more accurately characterized by a child running into the street without looking first.)

11. Easily loses things such as pencils, tools, papers, etc., which may be necessary to complete school or other work.
12. Interrupts others inappropriately, butting in when not invited.
13. Talks impulsively or excessively.
14. Others report that the person doesn't seem to be listening when spoken to.

The three caveats on these diagnostic criteria are that the behaviors must have started before age seven, not represent some other form of classifiable mental illness, and occur more frequently than the average person of the same age. The term ADHD-RS, the RS representing Residual State, is used to describe this condition in adults.

CONDITIONS THAT MAY MIMIC ADD, AND VICE-VERSA

Several conditions may mimic certain characteristics of ADD, causing an inaccurate diagnosis. These include:

❖ **Anxiety disorders.** ADD may cause anxiety when people find themselves in school, life, or work situations with which they cannot cope. ADD differs from garden-variety anxiety disorder in that an anxiety disorder is usually episodic, whereas ADD is continual and lifelong. If anxiety comes and goes, it's probably not ADD.

❖ **Depression.** ADD may also cause depression, and sometimes depression causes a high level of distractibility that's diagnosed as ADD. Depression, however, is also usually episodic. When depressed patients are given Ritalin or other stimulant drugs, which seem to help with ADD patients, depressed patients will often experience a short-term "high" followed by an even more severe rebound-depression.

❖ **Manic-Depressive Illness.** Manic-depression is not often diagnosed as ADD because the classic symptoms of manic-depressive illness are so severe. One day a person is renting a ballroom in a hotel to entertain all his friends; the next day he's suicidal. Yet ADD is often misdiagnosed as manic-depressive illness. A visit to any adult-ADD support group usually produces several first-person stories of ADD adults who were given lithium or some other inappropriate drug because their ADD was misdiagnosed as manic-depressive illness.

❖ **Seasonal Affective Disorder.** This recently discovered condition appears to be related to a deficiency of sunlight exposure during the winter months and is most prevalent in northern latitudes. Seasonal affective disorder (SAD) symptoms include depression, lethargy, and a lack of concentration during the winter months. It's historically cyclical, predictable, and is currently treated by shining a certain spectrum and brightness of light on a person for a few minutes or hours at a particular time each day, tricking the body into thinking that the longer days of spring and summer have arrived. Seasonal affective disorder is sometimes misdiagnosed as ADD, and vice versa, but seasonality is its hallmark trait.

MAKING A DIAGNOSIS

Most likely, looking at the American Psychiatric Association's criteria, you saw bits of yourself and others. While numerous books and therapists offer elaborate (and sometimes expensive) tests for ADHD/ADD, it's important to remember that, according to the American Psychiatric Association, the only true diagnostic standard is to "hit" on their specified criteria, viewed through the lens of their three caveats. While elaborate and time-consuming tests may be interesting, and may provide useful insights into other facets of personality, none are officially recognized by the American Psychiatric Association, which is the final arbiter of these matters in the United States.

This is important for the consumer to realize, since some practitioners or clinic managers state that a diagnosis of ADD requires that you pay them for a test. Such is not the case.

❖ **The Hallowell-Ratey criteria.** In 1992, psychiatrists Edward M. Hallowell and John J. Ratey developed, through years of clinical practice, study, and observation, their own set of criteria for spotting probable ADD, particularly in adults. While this isn't an "official" set of diagnostic criteria, since its first appearance in their book *Driven to Distraction* it has become one of the more common standards against which both lay people and clinicians measure the probability of a person having ADD.

In publishing this, they added this caveat: *The following criteria are suggested only. They are based upon our clinical experience and constitute what we consider to be the most commonly encountered symptoms in adults with Attention Deficit Disorder. These criteria have not been validated by field trials, and should be regarded only as a clinical guide. Consider a criterion as being met only if the behavior is considerably more frequent than that of most people of the same mental age.*

According to Hallowell and Ratey, ADD may be present when we see a chronic disturbance in which at least twelve of the following criteria are present (quoted from *Driven to Distraction: Recognizing and Coping with Attention Deficit Disorder from Childhood through Adulthood* [*Simon & Schuster, 1995*] *with the kind permission of the authors*):

1. **A sense of underachievement, of not meeting one's goals (regardless of how much one has actually accomplished).** We put this symptom first because it is the most common reason an adult seeks help. "I just can't get my act together" is the frequent refrain. The person may be highly accomplished by objective standards, or may be floundering, stuck with a sense of being lost in a maze, unable to capitalize on innate potential.

2. **Difficulty getting organized.** Organization is a major problem for most adults with ADD. Without the structure of school, without parents around to get things organized for him or her, the adult may stagger under the organizational demand of everyday life. The supposed "little things" may mount up to create huge obstacles. For want of the proverbial nail—a missed appointment, a lost check, a forgotten deadline—their kingdom may be lost.

3. **Chronic procrastination or trouble beginning a task.** Often, due to their fears that they won't do it right, they put it off, and off, which, of course, only adds to the anxiety around the task.

4. **Many projects going simultaneously; trouble with follow-through.** A corollary of #3. As one task is put off, another is taken up. By the end of the day, week, or year, countless projects have been undertaken, while few have found completion.

5. **Tendency to say what comes to mind without necessarily considering the timing or appropriate-**

ness of the remark. Like the child with ADD in the classroom, the adult with ADD gets carried away in enthusiasm. An idea comes and it must be spoken; tact or guile yields to child-like exuberance.

6. **A restive search for high stimulation**. The adult with ADD is always on the lookout for something novel, something engaging, something in the outside world that can catch up with the whirlwind that's rushing inside.

7. **A tendency to be easily bored**. A corollary of #6. Boredom surrounds the adult with ADD like a sink-hole, ever ready to drain off energy and leave the individual hungry for more stimulation. This can easily be misinterpreted as a lack of interest; actually it is a relative inability to sustain interest over time. As much as the person cares, his battery pack runs low quickly.

8. **Easy distractibility, trouble focusing attention, tendency to tune out or drift away in the middle of a page or a conversation, often coupled with an ability to hyperfocus at times**. The hallmark symptom of ADD. The "tuning out" is quite involuntary. It happens when the person isn't looking, so to speak, and the next thing you know, he or she isn't there. An often extraordinary ability to hyperfocus is also usually present, emphasizing the fact that this is a syndrome not of attention deficit but of attention inconsistency.

9. **Often creative, intuitive, highly intelligent**. Not a symptom, but a trait deserving of mention. Adults with ADD often have unusually creative minds. In the midst of their disorganization and distractibility, they show flashes of brilliance. Capturing this "special something" is one of the goals of treatment.

10. **Trouble in going through established channels, following proper procedure**. Contrary to how it

often appears, this is not due to some unresolved problem with authority figures. Rather, it is a manifestation of boredom and frustration: boredom with routine ways of doing things and excitement around novel approaches, and frustration with being unable to do things the way they're supposed to be done.

11. **Impatient; low tolerance for frustration**. Frustration of any sort reminds the adult with ADD of all the failures in the past. "Oh, no," he thinks, "here we go again." So he gets angry or withdraws. The impatience has to do with the need for stimulation and can lead others to think of the individual as immature or insatiable.

12. **Impulsive, either verbally or in action, as in** impulsive spending of money, changing plans, enacting new schemes or career plans, and the like. This is one of the more dangerous of the adult symptoms, or, depending on the impulse, one of the more advantageous.

13. **Tendency to worry needlessly, endlessly; tendency to scan the horizon looking for something to worry about alternating with inattention to or disregard for actual dangers.** Worry is what attention turns into when it isn't focused on some task.

14. **Sense of impending doom, insecurity, alternating with high-risk-taking.** This symptom is related to both the tendency to worry needlessly and the tendency to be impulsive.

15. **Mood swings, depression, especially when disengaged from a person or a project.** Adults with ADD, more than children, are given to unstable moods. Much of this is due to their experience of frustration and/or failure, while some of it is due to the biology of the disorder.

16. **Restlessness.** One usually does not see in an adult the full-blown hyperactivity one may see in a

child. Instead one sees what looks like "nervous energy:" pacing, drumming of fingers, shifting position while sitting, leaving a table or room frequently, feeling edgy while at rest.

17. **Tendency toward addictive behavior.** The addiction may be to a substance such as alcohol or cocaine, or to an activity, such as gambling, or shopping, or eating, or overwork.

18. **Chronic problems with self-esteem.** These are the direct and unhappy result of years of conditioning: years of being told one is a klutz, a space-shot, an underachiever, lazy, weird, different, out of it, and the like. Years of frustration, failure, or of just not getting it right do lead to problems with self-esteem. What is impressive is how resilient most adults are, despite all setbacks.

19. **Inaccurate self-observation**. People with ADD are poor self-observers. They do not accurately gauge the impact they have on other people. This can often lead to big misunderstandings and deeply hurt feelings.

20. **Family history of ADD or manic-depressive illness or depression or substance abuse or other disorders of impulse control or mood.** Since ADD is genetically transmitted and related to the other conditions mentioned, it is not uncommon (but not necessary) to find such a family history.

In addition to requiring 12 out of 20 hits on this test, Drs. Hallowell and Ratey add that, as with the DSM criteria, these characteristics must include a childhood history of similar behaviors and not be explainable by other medical or psychiatric conditions.

The DSM says a psychiatric diagnosis isn't warranted unless something's wrong—unless there's some significant impairment of a major life function. My friend and editor, Dave deBronkart, found that he meets the criteria for ADD on the above tests. When he told an ADD expert that he was quite successful in his life nonetheless, the response was, "You probably have something wrong with you and don't even know it."

This is symptomatic of how pathology-obsessed our culture has become, often to the disadvantage of people (particularly children) who are forced to wear the label of "something wrong."

In contrast, this book offers new insights, perspectives, and tools that many find useful and compatible additions to the traditional view of ADD.

"As a physician I've worked among indigenous hunting societies in other parts of the world, from Asia to the Americas. Over and over again I see among their adults and children the constellation of behaviors that we call ADD.

"Among the members of the tribes of northern Canada, such as the caribou hunters of the McKenzie Basin, these adaptive characteristics—constantly scanning the environment, quick decision-making (impulsiveness) and a willingness to take risks—contribute every year to the tribe's survival.

"These same behaviors, however, often make it difficult for tribal children to succeed in western schools when we try to impose our western curriculum on them."

—Will Krynen, MD

Chapter Three

■■■■

Hunters in Our Schools and Offices: The Origin of ADD

There is a passion for hunting, something deeply implanted in the human breast.
— Charles Dickens (*Oliver Twist*, 1837)

The earliest theories about attention deficit disorder characterized it as a diseased state which had to do with brain damage or dysfunction. At various times it has been lumped in with fetal alcohol syndrome, mental retardation, various genetic mental illnesses, psychiatric disorders resulting from early trauma or childhood abuse, and the theory that parental smoking led to fetal oxygen deprivation.

Prior to the early 1970s, when ADD was first characterized as a specific disorder, ADD children and adults were largely treated simply as "bad people" (even though attentional deficits have been recognized in the psychological literature since 1905). They were

21

the kids who always got into trouble, the James Deans of the world, the rootless and unsettled adults like Abraham Lincoln's father, The Lone Ranger, or John Dillinger.

More recent research, however, has demonstrated a high incidence of ADD among the parents of ADD children. This discovery caused some psychologists to initially postulate that ADD was the result of growing up in a dysfunctional family; they suggested that ADD may follow the same pattern as child or spousal abuse, moving through generations as learned behavior. The dietary-cause advocates contended that children pattern their parent's eating habits, and this accounts for the generational patterns of ADD. Other studies suggest that, like Down's Syndrome or muscular dystrophy, ADD is a genetic disease, and a specific gene* has been identified by scientists as the leading candidate.

But if ADD is a genetic disease or an abnormality, it's a popular one, possibly afflicting as many as 25 million individuals in the United States. (Some estimates put ADD as occurring in 20 percent of males and 5 percent of females. Other estimates are much lower, hitting a bottom of 3 percent of males and .5 percent of females.) With such a wide distribution among our population, is it reasonable to assume that ADD is simply a quirk? That it's some sort of an aberration caused by defective genes or child abuse?

When the condition is so widely distributed, inevitable questions arise: *Why? Where did ADD come from?*

The answer is: people with ADD are the leftover

---

* The A1 variant of the D2 dopamine receptor gene

hunters, those whose ancestors evolved and matured thousands of years in the past in hunting societies.

There is ample precedent for genetic "diseases" which, in fact, represent evolutionary survival strategies. Sickle-cell anemia, for example, is now known to make its victims less susceptible to malaria. When living in the jungles of Africa where malaria is endemic, it was a powerful evolutionary tool against death by disease; in the malaria-free environment of North America, it became a liability.

The same is true of Tay-Sachs disease, a genetic condition which hits mainly Eastern European Jews, and confers on them a relative immunity to tuberculosis. And even cystic fibrosis, the deadly genetic disease common among Caucasians (one in twenty-five white Americans carries the gene), may represent a genetic adaptation—recent research indicates the cystic fibrosis gene helps protect its victims, at younger ages, from death by such diarrheal diseases as cholera, which periodically swept Europe thousands of years ago.

It's not so unusual, apparently, for humans to have, built into our genetic material, protection against local diseases and other environmental conditions. Certainly, Darwin's theory of natural selection argues in favor of such bodily defenses. Those individuals with the immunities would survive to procreate and pass along their genetic material.

As the human race moved from its earliest ancestors, two basic types of cultures evolved. In the areas which were lush with plant and animal life and had a low human population density, hunters and gatherers predominated. In other parts of the world (particularly Asia), farming or agricultural societies evolved.

SUCCESSFUL HUNTERS

Be it pursuing buffalo in North America, hunting deer in Europe, chasing wildebeest in Africa, or picking fish from a stream in Asia, these hunters needed a certain set of physical and mental characteristics to be successful:

❖ **They constantly monitor their environment.** That rustle in the bushes could be a lion or a coiled snake. Failure to be fully aware of the environment and notice the faint sound might mean a swift and painful death. Or, that sound or flash of movement might be the animal the hunter was stalking, and noticing it could mean the difference between a full belly and hunger.

I've walked through forests and jungles with modern Hunter-types, in the United States, Europe, and East Africa, and one characteristic always struck me: they notice everything. A flipped-over stone, a tiny footprint, a distant sound, an odd smell in the air, the direction in which flowers point or moss grows. All these things have meaning to Hunters and, even when walking quickly, they notice *everything*..

❖ **They can totally throw themselves into the hunt; time is elastic.** Another characteristic of a good Hunter is the ability to totally focus on the moment, utterly abandoning all consideration of any other time or place. When the Hunter sees the prey he gives chase through gully or ravine, over fields or through trees, giving no thought to the events of the day before, not considering the future, simply living totally in that one pure moment and immersing himself in it. When involved in the hunt, time seems to speed; when not in the hunt, time becomes slow. While a Hunter's ability to concentrate in general may be low, his ability to utterly throw himself into the hunt *at the moment* is astonishing.

❖ **They're flexible, capable of changing strategy on a moment's notice.** If the wild boar vanishes into the brush, and a rabbit appears, the Hunter is off in a new direction. Orderliness is not particularly important to a Hunter, but the abilities to make a quick decision and then act on it are vital.

❖ **They can throw an incredible burst of energy into the hunt,** so much so that they often injure themselves or exceed "normal" capabilities, without realizing it until later. Not unlike that quintessential of all Hunters, the lion, they have incredible bursts of energy—but not necessarily a lot of staying power. Given the choice of describing themselves as the tortoise or the hare in Aesop's famous fable, a Hunter would always say that he or she is the hare.

❖ **They think visually.** Hunters often describe their actions in terms of pictures, rather than words or feelings. They create outlines in their heads of where they've been and where they're going. (Aristotle taught a memory method like this, with which a person would visualize rooms in a house, then objects in the rooms. When he gave a speech, he'd simply move from room to room in his memory, noticing the objects therein, which were reminders of the next thing he had to talk about.) Hunters often aren't much interested in abstractions, or else want to convert them to a visual form as quickly as possible. They tend to be lousy chess players, disdaining strategy because they prefer to go straight for the jugular.

❖ **They love the hunt, but are easily bored by mundane tasks** such as having to clean the fish, dress the meat, or fill out the paperwork. Donald Haughey, a former senior executive with Holiday Inns, tells the story of how Kemmons Wilson, the legendary founder of Holiday Inns, had a group of executives he called Bear Skinners. Wilson would go out into the world and shoot the bear (negotiate a new hotel site, bring in new financing, open a new division, etc.), and his Bear Skinners would take care of the details of "skinning and cleaning" the deal.

❖ **They'll face danger that "normal" individuals would avoid.** A wounded boar, or elephant, or bear, can kill you—and many a Hunter has been killed by his would-be prey. If you extend this analogy to warfare, where the Hunters are often the front line infantry or the most aggressive officers, the same is true. Hunters take risks. Extending this metaphor, Patton was a Hunter, Marshall a Farmer.

❖ **They're hard on themselves and those around them.** When your life depends on split-second decisions, your frustration and impatience threshold necessarily tend to be low. A fellow Hunter who doesn't get out of the way of a shot, or a soldier who defies orders and smokes on a dark night showing the enemy your position, cannot be tolerated.

PEOPLE WITH ADD ARE DESCENDANTS OF HUNTERS

So, the question: where did ADD come from? If you compare the list of classic ADD symptoms, and the list of the characteristics of a good hunter, you'll see that they match almost perfectly. In other words, an individual with the ADD collection of characteristics would make an extraordinarily good hunter. A failure to have any one of those characteristics might mean death in the forest or jungle.

Chapter Four

"Normal" People: The Origins of Agriculture

When tillage begins, other arts follow. The farmers therefore are the founders of human civilization.
—Daniel Webster (*On Agriculture*, January 13, 1840)

Since ADD is a collection of skills and predilections necessary for the success and survival of a good Hunter, we're left with the question, "What about non-ADD people?" Where did their skills evolve from, and why do they represent the majority of the people in our culture?

The answer lies with the second basic type of human culture which primitive man produced: the agricultural society. In this sort of community, farmers were the ones who provided sustenance and survival. And the skills of a good Farmer are quite different from those of a good Hunter.

To go through a list parallel to those of a Hunter, we find that a good Farmer:

❖ **Isn't easily distracted by his or her environment.** It may take three or four weeks to plant all the

27

seed or rice shoots necessary for a complete crop, and the window of good weather may be very limited. If the Farmer were to be distracted while planting, and wander off to investigate a noise in the forest, or spend days trying to figure out why one plant was slightly larger than another, the crop wouldn't get planted—and he or she would starve.

❖ **Farmers sustain a slow-and-steady effort** for hours every day, days every week, weeks every month. While it could be argued that there are bursts of energy needed during harvest time, most Hunters would say that such bursts are nothing compared to chasing a deer fifteen miles through a forest. And the Farmer's bursts need to last all day, often for days or weeks at a time. Even in high gear, a Farmer's efforts would be characterized as fast-and-steady.

❖ **Farmers see the long-range picture,** and stick to it. While subtle or limited experiments are useful for Farmers, to bet the entire crop on a new seed might lead to disaster. A Farmer isn't looking five minutes ahead, or an hour ahead (like a Hunter), but must, instead, look years ahead. How will this crop affect the soil? What impact will it have on erosion? Will it be enough to sustain the family or village through the winter? I've visited terraced hillsides supporting rice paddies or olive trees built by long-sighted farmers in Israel, Greece, and China that are still farmed more than 3,000 years after they were constructed: Farmers have the long view.

❖ **Farmers are not easily bored.** They pace themselves when living, the same way they pace themselves when farming. During the summer when things are growing, or during the winter when not much can be done, farmers find constructive tasks to occupy their time such as building furniture, chopping firewood, or weeding the garden. They don't mind repetitive tasks or things that take a long time to accomplish because that's the nature of farming. Given Aesop's model, a farmer would describe him or herself as the tortoise who ultimately wins the race through slow and steady effort.

❖ **Farmers are team players,** and often very sensitive to others' needs and feelings. Because Farmers often must live and work together, particularly in primitive farming communities, they must cooperate. Japanese society is perhaps the most exaggerated example of this, evolving from an almost purely agricultural base. They think in terms of abstract notions and feelings, considering the future and the good of the community, and are patient chess players. Teamwork is a powerful asset of a Farmer.

❖ **Farmers attend to the details.** A Farmer must make sure all the wheat is threshed, all the cows are milked completely, all the fields are planted, or he or she courts disaster for the entire community. If a cow isn't milked completely it can become infected; a crop put into ground that's too wet or too dry might rot or wither. Einstein's "God is in the details" might be a favorite saying of a farmer.

❖ **Farmers are cautious.** Farming doesn't often demand that a person face short-term danger. Farmers learn, instead, to face the more long-term dangers. They're often better planners than they are fighters.

❖ **Farmers are patient with others.** The patience that it takes to watch a plant grow for five months is easily translated into patience with a co-worker who wants to explain a problem or situation.

FARMERS AS NON-ADD INDIVIDUALS

A quick review of the Farmer's characteristics (obviously simplified for purposes of explanation), and a comparison of them with the Hunter's skills, shows that one could easily recharacterize ADD and non-ADD persons as Hunters and Farmers. Although most people don't fit into such neat categories, it's still possible to see the archetypes demonstrated in people we all know.

Individuals who are almost pure Hunters are classified as classic ADD. Individuals who are almost pure Farmers are classified as slow, careful, methodical, and, sometimes, boring. Since Farmer characteristics are less likely to be risky and dangerous (for reasons explained), these extremely non-ADD people are not often classified by psychologists. They don't get into trouble, and tend not to stand out in our society.

Accepting the idea that there's probably a bell curve to these behaviors, though, we can posit a norm which incorporates both Hunter and Farmer behaviors, with swings in both directions on either side of the center line.

An interesting footnote to this hypothesis is the observation that Europeans often view Americans and Australians as "brash and risk-taking." Americans and Australians often view Europeans as "stodgy and conservative." Accepting the notion that ADD is an inherited trait, consider the types of people who would risk life and limb for a journey across the Atlantic in the seventeenth century—they'd have to be either desperate Farmers or normal Hunters. Similarly, Australia's early white population was often descended from prisoners sent there by England; the misfits and malcontents of British society. (I suspect a very large percentage were ADD Hunters who couldn't succeed as the Industrial Revolution "Farmer-ized" the British labor market and culture.)

ADD also appears to be a condition that's relatively rare among Japanese whose ancestors have lived in a purely agricultural society for at least 6,000 years.

A final postscript: Some people have objected to the words Hunter and Farmer. Hunter, some say, has negative connotations: killer, predator, a threat in the night. Farmer is equally negative, in that it implies a boring, passive sort of person, and many Farmers (as described in this book) are far from either.

If it makes you more comfortable, perhaps an alternate set of words would be Lookout and Cultivator. *Both are necessary for the common good:* Where would the cultivator be without the lookout, and vice versa?

Worse, think what a disaster it would be to put either in the other's job. The Cultivator doesn't catch the little signs of the impending invasion, and the Lookout can't pay attention long enough to weed the garden.

Yet that's precisely what happens to most ADD Lookouts in today's classrooms and offices. If they look out the window (as their instincts demand), they're scolded for not being good, attentive Farmers.

A more successful approach might be to recognize and speak to the skills inherent in the fast-moving Lookout frame of mind. This may require a shift in viewpoint, but it's not difficult once you see the difference between Hunters and Farmers.

Chapter Five

—

Could Someone With ADD Have Survived in a Primitive Hunting Society?

Insanity in individuals is something rare— but in groups, parties and nations, and epochs it is the rule.
— Nietzsche, *Beyond Good and Evil*

Many thoughtful people on all sides of the ADD issue have asked me this question. One of the most articulate put it quite succinctly when he said that if he'd been alive 10,000 years ago he would have been doomed because "I'd forget to take my spear with me when we left for the hunt!"

Others have taken pains to point out to me the necessity of organized cooperative action for most primitive hunting parties. The ideal of a hyperactive loner going through the woods looking for dinner doesn't at all characterize how most anthropologists describe primitive (or today's) hunter/gatherer methods.

At first glance, it would appear that these considerations blow a hole in the hypothesis that modern people with ADD are carrying around a remnant of hunter/gatherer genetic material. It lends credibility to the notion that ADD is, in fact, a "disease" or at least "not normal," and may not have ever been "normal" in human history.

But that overlooks a critical issue: cultural context, the effect of what we learn to believe about ourselves as we're growing up.

Cultural anthropologists are quick to point out that it's extremely difficult for any one culture to clearly view another. We instinctively assume when observing their behaviors that they're motivated in the same ways we are, that they behave the way they do for the same reasons we would if we were in their situation, and that they share our assumptions about how the world works and humanity's role in the world.

This is a dangerous error, which even tripped up Margaret Mead when she was writing *Coming of Age in Samoa.* Since her well-intentioned but well-publicized error, few anthropologists would make this mistake. But it's easy for somebody untrained in the field.

The problem, essentially, is that most people, when thinking of "primitive times," imagine *themselves* running around in the woods wearing animal skins and carrying a spear. In their mind's eye, they transport a twentieth century person back into a fantasy past. But these "Connecticut Yankees in King Arthur's Court" don't represent what it was like to grow up in those times; they arrive in a different era complete with all our acculturation, carrying along all the damage done to them by our culture. They haul along the preparations we've received for a Farmers/Industrialists life, but utterly lacking preparation for a Hunters/Gatherers life.

The fact of the matter is that people in hunter/gatherer tribes live very different lives than we do, and therefore grow up to be very different persons from us.

ADDERS ARE DAMAGED BY GROWING UP IN OUR SOCIETY, NOT IN HUNTING CULTURES

Cultural anthropologist Jay Fikes pointed this out to me when we first discussed the idea of hunters and farmers as an explanation for many modern psychological differences among people. His research showed that individuals living among the historically agricultural Native Americans, such as the Hopi and other Pueblo Indians, are relatively sedate and risk-averse. On the other hand, Fikes said, members of the hunting tribes such as the Navajo are "constantly scanning their environment and are more immediately sensitive to nuances. They're also the ultimate risk takers. They and the Apaches were great raiders and warriors."

Navajo children grow up in a society of Navajo hunter and warrior adults (at least they did before we conquered them, destroyed their culture, shattered their religions, stole their land, and murdered most of their citizens). The Navajo raised their children as hunters and warriors. Until we arrived with horses and guns, they were extraordinarily successful, and had survived as an intact culture for thousands of years longer than we have.

But we today are not a society of hunters, raiders, and warriors. We are farmers, office- and factory-workers. Therefore, we punish and discourage hunter and warrior behavior in our children and adults.

When people grow up being punished for being the way they are, they become damaged. They think of themselves as misfits and incompetents. They lose their own personal power, become shaken and fearful, and develop a variety of compensating behaviors—many of which are less than useful.

What you—the parent, teacher, counselor, or physician—tell the ADD child about himself can have a decisive effect. Children respond very differently to being told "This is how your brain works" instead of "Your brain just don't work right."

To think that these modern ADD people—damaged, shaken, hurt, and weakened by growing up in the wrong time and culture—could somehow solve all their problems by simply transporting themselves back to some mythical prehistoric hunting era is a fantasy. It wouldn't work. They weren't raised and trained to survive in that environment; they weren't taught to channel their energies into being hunters and warriors. Instead, they were spanked and slapped, told to shut up and given detention, and—the ultimate insult—told that they are damaged goods and have a brain disease worthy of the labels "deficit" and "disorder."

HUNTERS ARE BOTH BORN AND MADE

Every type of culture puts enormous amounts of effort into educating and inculcating cultural values into their citizens. That's how it becomes a culture.

In hundreds of ways, we are daily taught and reminded of what is expected of us, what the limits and boundaries are, and what are appropriate and inappropriate goals and behaviors. Most of this teaching is so subtle we're totally unaware of it—a glance from a stranger when we talk too loud in a restaurant, for example—but our days are filled with it. It shapes us and molds our beliefs, our assumptions, and ultimately our reality.

We come face-to-face with these differences when we encounter other cultures. I remember my shock and dismay at discovering, the first time I was in Japan negotiating on behalf of my company, that I had committed dozens of major cultural blunders in my interactions. Even more shocking confrontations occur when we meet people from far disparate tribes: I remember how odd I felt when, deep in the jungle of central Uganda, I stood in a village of people who were mostly naked. My jeans, shoes, shirt, and carried jacket seemed an oddity to them, and began to seem that way to me after a few hours.

And so we train our young. We reinforce and strengthen in them those behaviors, assumptions, and beliefs that we find useful as a society, and we discourage or crush in them those that are not useful or even counterproductive to the orderly flow of our culture and its work.

Farming societies teach their young how to be good farmers. Hunting societies train their children in the ways of the hunt. Industrial societies raise their children to be good factory workers. Warrior cultures teach warfare to their children.

By the time a young man in the Ugandan Ik hunter/gatherer tribe is ready to go out on a hunt with the men, he has been trained his entire life for that moment. He's played at it virtually from birth. He's had a personal mentor for half his lifetime, an adult who has taught him the lore of the jungle and the prey. He's practiced for thousands of hours. He may be high-energy, impulsive, distractible, and a risk-taker, but he is also a brilliant and proficient hunter, a master killing machine. He has been trained from his first steps to focus and concentrate that wild energy on this one task, and to exploit and use his scanning and quick-thinking and love of adventure to cooperate with the other men in the jungle to bring home dinner.

In this context, you can see how naïve it is to ask if a "person with ADD" (which is, after all, a "disorder" defined only by, and unique to, our culture) could succeed in a hunting/gathering society.

There's little doubt that a child who's had his ego bashed from thirty different directions since he was little, who's spent his life being told "don't be that way" and "sit down and shut up," whose only well-honed hunting skill is finding MTV with his remote control, would fail in the jungle. Anyone who's always been told they're no good will lack confidence and will fail to perform.

This was perfectly illustrated by a story in *Newsweek* in 1994. It was an account of an ongoing study of a group of now-adults with ADD who were diagnosed as having ADD in elementary school in the 1960s: some had significantly lower outcomes in life than people not diagnosed with ADD.

But nowhere in the study, or the article, was it mentioned that only the ADD subjects were told they were "disordered" and required to take drugs for their "mind sickness" while still children.

For the study to have statistical validity, a matching population of non-ADD children would have to have been treated the same way, and their outcome would have to be compared against the ADD population.

Of course no ethical researcher would dare take a perfectly ordinary child and tell him such things: too many past studies in the field of psychology have shown how destructive the outcome could be. But that's exactly what we've been doing with our ADD children.

If that same child with the bashed ego had been born into a hunting tribe, so that his traits were developed instead of being beaten out of him, he may well have turned out to be the mightiest of their warriors, the most brilliant of their hunters, the wisest of their elders.

Chapter Six

━

How to Turn a "Disorder" Back into a Skill
(A Survival Guide for ADD Adults)

Nearly every man who develops an idea works it up to the point where it looks impossible, and then he gets discouraged. That's not the place to become discouraged.   — Thomas Edison

If you've read this far with an open mind, I hope you've accepted the notion that ADD is neither a deficit nor a disorder. It is, instead, an inherited set of skills, abilities, and personality tendencies which would enable a Hunter or warrior or lookout to be eminently success-ful—and would condemn a Farmer or an accountant to certain disaster. So how did this powerful set of Hunter skills come to be labeled as a disorder?

Historically, societies have viewed people whose behaviors they didn't understand, or which weren't "the norm," as inferior. Certainly the debates of the seventeenth, eighteenth, and nineteenth centuries here

41

in the United States about whether Native Americans and African slaves were human highlights the extremes to which people are willing to take notions of culturalism. People who are seen as different are often lumped into a "not-quite-human" category, as were Japanese-Americans during World War II or physically disabled Americans in present times.

The following quotation serves as example to this phenomenon: *"I am not, nor ever have been, in favor of bringing about in any way the social and political equality of the white and black races ... I am not nor ever have been in favor of making voters or jurors of Negroes, nor of qualifying them to hold office, nor to intermarry with white people; and I will say in addition to this that there is a physical difference between the races which I believe will for ever forbid the two races living together on terms of social and political equality."* (—Abraham Lincoln)

Therefore, when Hunter-type children were put into Farmer-model schools and failed, it was a logical next step to "find out what's wrong with them." Clearly, the logic went, it couldn't be the school that was at fault—some children were graduating with honors. That demonstrated the viability of the traditional, modern, (underfunded, overworked) school system.

Unfortunately, it doesn't necessarily hold true, as educators from Horace Mann to Rudolph Steiner have historically pointed out.

Very few pure Hunter societies remain on the planet, and none of them thrive as a primary culture within the industrialized world. Most modern jobs require a Farmer mentality—show up for work at a certain time, do a task for a certain number of hours, and end the day in time to rest and prepare for the next day. Put this bolt on that wheel, over and over. Meet with these people, understand that concept, move this paper from desk A to desk B and then back.

Our schools, too, are set up along Farmer lines. Sit quietly at the desk, children are told, while the teacher talks and points to pages in the book. Ignore that child next to you who's sniffling; don't rattle your papers; don't look ahead in the book.

To a smart Hunter with a low boredom threshold, this is torture! It's a prescription for failure.

And, as our schools continue to suffer from a lack of funding and classrooms continue to increase in size, so do the number of distractions. In a 15-child classroom, an ADD child may have few problems that can't be dealt with directly by the teacher. But as our schools are placed under the increasing burden of underfunding and teacher-overload/overwork, Hunter children are increasingly being noticed. As a result there seems to be a rather sudden "epidemic" of ADD.

So the kids are doing poorly in school, they're bored and acting out. The teacher figures there must be something wrong with the children. Along come the diagnostic Farmers of the psychological industry, and—presto—a new "disorder" is discovered!

This is not to say that Hunters don't have short attention spans. Far from it—they certainly do. But they have any number of compensating characteristics, such as voracious curiosity, continual scanning of the environment, and broad-based interest. If our schools and jobs were structured to allow for the expression of these characteristics, ADD might become as irrelevant a medical classification as is its reciprocal, the extreme Farmer end of the bell curve. (In a later chapter we refer to the latter as TSDD or "task-switching deficit disorder"; it's classified in medical literature as the "overfocusing syndrome.")

Unfortunately, such a utopian notion is extremely unlikely. Employers aren't about to change businesses to accommodate the Hunters in our society (although there are many jobs ideally suited, as they stand, for Hunters). And it's equally unlikely that America's schools will quickly change the structure of classrooms—despite the fact that more than 3 million American schoolchildren are on Ritalin (often at the urging of teachers) to medicate Hunters into behaving like Farmers.

So, what's an adult Hunter to do in a Farmer's world?

The easiest, most obvious, and least stressful solution is to find a Hunter job that makes use of hunting skills. Police officers, private detectives, freelance writers, reporters, airplane pilots, spies (hopefully for our side), military combat personnel, disc jockeys, salespeople, consultants, and the thousands of varieties of entrepreneurs—all have a very high percentage of Hunters among their ranks. One of the happiest Hunters I ever knew was an old man who lived in the woods of northern Michigan and made his living as...a hunter. Five wives had come and gone, but the "Old Man" as we all called him (and he called himself) would never divorce himself from his traps and guns.

If one is capable and willing to sit through the years of school necessary to get the professional credentials, there are many opportunities for Hunters among the professions, as well. Trial lawyers are often Hunters (and usually have a good, solid Farmer as a research assistant). In medicine, the areas of surgery and trauma care seem to draw the excitement- and challenge-craving Hunters. In business, when hooked up with a supportive Farmer assistant, Hunters often make excellent senior executives (read the biographies of William Randolph Hearst or Malcolm Forbes, for examples), particularly when their position requires a large reservoir of creativity and willingness to take risks—two of the cardinal characteristics of Hunters. For these same reasons, we see many politicians who are apparently Hunters (JFK is a probable example), and William F. Buckley's autobiography, *Overdrive*, is a wonderful description of the life experience of a man who, while he may not be a Hunter, certainly embodies the energy level and love of stimulation and new experience common to Hunters:

> (*I have the whole morning clear, which is good because there is a speech right after lunch at the Waldorf, which has to be thought through, as the occasion doesn't permit a regular lecture. I am to speak for only twenty minutes. I look at the assignment and calculate the time it will take to prepare for it—say a half hour, leaning on familiar material. I have found that one can work with special concentration when hard up against that kind of a deadline. I have time left to attack the briefcase.* —page 100 of Buckley's *Overdrive*)

If you're a Hunter stuck with a Farmer job, there are simple behavioral changes you can make, in order to increase your probability for success in a Farmer's world:

❖**Organize your time around tasks.** Hunters tend to do well with short bursts of high-quality effort and attention. So, taking large jobs and breaking them into small components is a useful first step. "Pigeonhole" your jobs. (More detail about this in the next chapter.)

❖ **Train your attention span.** Techniques like meditation have been around forever, and Hunters are often drawn to them. They enjoy silence—in little chunks—because it turns off the distractions for a few minutes and allows them to relax. While many Farmers crave continual stimulation—the radio is on at the office while they're doing their work—such distractions make it almost impossible for many Hunters to work productively.

While Hunters will probably never be able to train themselves to totally ignore distractions (it's a survival skill that's hard-wired into Hunters), experience demonstrates that it is possible to learn to more powerfully direct their attention to a single item, task, or time. The literature of Transcendental Meditation is full of such studies, and many Hunters report that, while meditation was difficult at first, it became an important component of their lives once they made a habit of it.

There are many books and courses on meditation, both religious and non-religious, and many Hunters find them useful. Ask any Catholic who's performed the Rosary "meditation" at least ten minutes a day for a week or two about their experience. The ones I've interviewed say that it gave them vivid new insights into how their mind and attentional mechanisms worked, and strengthened their ability to focus on other things.

A technique taught by Tibetan Buddhist monks is called Vipassana, or mindfulness. Basically, it means you watch your own mind, and catch yourself when your attention wanders. Sit for ten minutes a day, focusing your eyes on a point on the wall or a distant tree or whatever, and, whenever you notice yourself thinking, simply say to yourself, "thinking ." By "noticing" your wandering attention, you'll bring your attention back on track more powerfully than any will-power or brute-force techniques. After a few weeks of daily practice, Hunters report that they can bring this skill of mindfulness into their work and daily lives.

Another facet of this training involves learning to convert words into pictures. The auditory-processing problem mentioned earlier is often a serious difficulty for Hunters, but is also one Hunters can train themselves to overcome. Practice making visual pictures of things while having conversations; create mental images of lists of things to do; visualize yourself doing things you commit to. And practice paying attention when people talk to you. Listen carefully.

❖ **Break your work (or home) responsibilities into specific "goal units."** Hunters tend to be task- or goal- oriented. Once a goal is reached, they go on to another one, with renewed enthusiasm and vigor. So, instead of viewing work as a life-long "if-I-can-just-get-through-this" ordeal, break each task into a set of short-term goals.

This week, write the marketing plan. Break it into pieces, and do each one a bit at a time. "Hunt" for success on a project-by-project basis, viewing each new item on your "to do" list as something to complete, scratch off, and leave behind.

Don't worry about next week, or the week after that. Break all your goals into short-term projects, and simply knock them down, one after another. At the end of the year, you'll discover that you reached your yearly goals and hardly noticed it.

❖ **Create "distraction-free zones."** Henry David Thoreau was so desperate to escape distraction in order to do his writing that he moved himself off to isolated Walden Pond. Organize your work space and time so you can create your own "Walden Pond." Close the door, turn off the radio, tell people to hold your calls, and work on one thing at a time. An hour a day in a "distraction-free zone" like this will often help a Hunter to literally double the output of work he or she could otherwise produce.

Because Hunters crave stimulation and thrive on distraction, this may seem like an alien concept at first. Moreover, some people are afraid that others will think they're just taking an hour to goof off. But those Hunters in the business world who have tried this (and there are many) report that it quickly becomes a powerful and regular habit, and that their peers are not generally bothered by it.

One ADD adult reported that, when in law school, he would rent a hotel room every Saturday in order to have a distraction-free place to "binge" his week's homework. This worked great to get him through school, but when he began to practice law, the distractions of the office made it impossible for him to accomplish anything meaningful. A secretary in a distant office dropping a pen would take his attention away from the work on which he was trying to concentrate. While this particular individual chose Ritalin as a way of shutting down his Lookout/Hunter ability, another option would have been to demand a private office and close the door. Unfortunately, in some workplaces, this is discouraged because it's interpreted as an effort to create "goofing-off time."

Another variation on creating a distraction-free

zone is to clean your desk at the end of every day, and to keep your living areas clean and organized. This is a survival skill that many Hunters have developed, because a messy desk or home represents such a multitude of distractions, it's nearly impossible to keep on a single task. Every time you start on one project, you notice out of the corner of your eye another thing on the desktop that needs attention ... and wander off-task.

It's interesting that most (but not all) adult Hunters I've interviewed report that they can only do "concentration" work when the room is absolutely silent or, if they're listening to music with no (distracting) words to it. This demand that the music be purely instrumental baffles many Farmer spouses or co-workers, but Hunters instantly recognize it as a sign of their personality type.

❖ **Exercise daily.** "If I don't run at least four times a week, I can't focus my attention worth a damn," a sales executive for an advertising agency told me recently. He is one of several Hunter adults who've reported that a half-hour to an hour of aerobic exercise "tunes" their brains nearly as well as Ritalin.

While there has been no research done on this particular area, the anecdotal evidence seems to support the notion that daily exercise—briskly walking a few miles, for example—increases blood flow to the brain, or somehow otherwise alters body chemistry in a way that increases focusing ability for Hunters. After all, if Hunters are biologically designed to hunt, then the daily "run after the prey" may well be a stimulant, or cause the release of hormones or neurotransmitters necessary for a Hunter's brain to work more smoothly.

❖ **Know what you do well, and stick to it—avoid Farmer tasks.** In over fifteen years of working periodically as a consultant to other businesses, I've met many Farmers who were successful entrepreneurs—but the majority were Hunters. It seems that the very definition of an entrepreneur is that of a Hunter.

On the other hand, I've also met many, many frustrated Hunter/entrepreneurs. The normal cycle seems to run like this:

1. The Hunter/entrepreneur comes up with a great business idea, and throws months or years into developing it. A business is produced, grows, and begins to prosper.

2. After a few years, the business reaches a size where the entrepreneur's responsibilities must shift from the "jump-start" phase (doing a little bit of everything, knowing all facets of the business, meddling in everybody's work), to the "middle management" phase. This is when an entrepreneurial venture becomes a company, usually when the organization expands to between six and fifteen employees.

At this point in the growth of a company, the Hunter skills that started the company become a liability in the head person. What the company needs now is solid, steady, carefully planned management—skills that are intrinsically unavailable to a Hunter. As a result, the company begins to falter, employees grow angry because they're not well-managed and their needs aren't being met, and the company gets jerked from new idea to new idea, with none ever becoming grounded in reality and solidified.

This is the point where most small businesses die. The reason is simple: Hunters can start companies, but they generally can't do a particularly good job of running them.

It's tragic that so many Hunters make the mistake

of trying to continue to run the businesses they started, when the appropriate thing at that stage in the life of a company is to bring in a competent Farmer as middle management, and turn the management of the business over to that Farmer. In this model, the Hunter/entrepreneur then becomes a "creative consultant" to the business, fills some traditional Hunter role in the company (such as sales), becomes the "chairperson" or overall "leader," or goes on to a new project.

I've seen some companies which have successfully navigated this hump point in the life of a business because the business was started as a partnership, where one partner was a Hunter and the other a Farmer. Often it's a husband-wife team, and after a few years one spouse ends up running the business, because he or she was the slow-and-steady Farmer, and those skills were needed at that point in the life of the business.

Hunters who are entrepreneurs must learn, if they want to be successful over the long term, to hire good Farmers, delegate both responsibility and authority to them, and not meddle. It's difficult and seems counterintuitive, but can produce solid success.

Some companies also intentionally pair up Hunters and Farmers as a team, particularly in the arena of sales. The Hunter goes out and gets the business, the Farmer does the paperwork and follow-through. And, of course, there is the classic model of the Hunter executive who would be totally lost without his or her Farmer secretary.

When preparing this manuscript I shared this chapter with a good friend, a Hunter who is a successful entrepreneur and consultant. He replied to me via electronic mail:

I betcha many Hunters, while excellent at their work, are terrible at management—I'm one. If my life depended on it, I doubt I could be good at the Farmer aspects of doing a budget, doing personnel reviews, or nurturing a department of dependable Farmers. I know. I tried for years, with a very good teacher. I wanted to succeed, I worked hard at it, but I hated it and failed and felt terrible as a result.

Being skilled but lacking the capacity to manage is enormously frustrating in a company where you can only move up by managing larger groups. In contrast, a few companies now recognize that some employees may be excellent at certain things without being good at (or interested in) managing or running a group. These companies identify a set of jobs that permit employees to advance to very high and respected positions without having to supervise.

Andrew Carnegie, a Hunter who came to America over 100 years ago with less than two dollars in his pocket and died one of the richest men in America, wrote for himself an epitaph which says: "Here lies one who knew how to get around him men who were cleverer than himself."

Chapter Seven

The Hunter's Struggle: Impulse and Its Control

I can resist everything except temptation.
    —Oscar Wilde, *Lady Windermere's Fan* (1892)

There are two characteristics of ADD which can seriously challenge a Hunter who is trying to be successful in life and society. They are *impulsivity* and *craving*.

These two characteristics are, in moderation, what make some Hunters incredibly successful in our society. Under control, these "driving forces" lead to the creation of institutions and businesses, to the writing of books and creation of art, to creative brainstorms that lead countries, companies, and lives in wholly new and wonderful directions.

When out of control, impulsivity and craving can drive a Hunter to self-destruction or prison. The two characteristics are closely interrelated.

❖ **Impulsivity** first manifests as the ability to make a quick decision, to sort through a lot of data

53

quickly and arrive at a conclusion. The problem is that the same burst of energy that a Hunter can bring to the hunt is brought to an impulsive decision. "Wow, yeah, let's do that!" which may lead to success in simple situations like a hunt in the woods, often leads to disaster in more complex worlds such as those of business. And, since the decision is usually followed by a burst of energy (designed by nature to help finish the hunt), Hunters often charge off in new, sometimes dangerous, directions.

Some Hunters create work environments for themselves where their impulsiveness is an asset. Thomas Edison had total control of his own time and work directions. And, it is said, he went off in more than 10,000 directions to try to make a light bulb which would work. Many professional writers, a common occupation of successful Hunters, have told me that they need the flexibility of controlling their own schedule so they can "burst work" when an inspiration or idea hits them.

On the other hand, for a Hunter in a Farmer job or school, impulsivity can lead to problems. Well-thought-out decisions are required in the work or business arenas, and impulsivity doesn't lend itself well to the thinking-out process. Successful Hunters get around impulsivity by several techniques:

❖ **Partner with a Farmer.** The combination of a Hunter and a Farmer can be frustrating for both, if neither is aware of the fundamental difference between the two in their world views and ways of working. Yet such a partnership is often a solid prescription for success if both *are* aware of their differences.

The Hunter is usually the "front man," the person who's most visible, fueling the business with creative genius and new ideas, trying innovative ways of doing things, and testing new directions. The Farmer has the dual job of "reality testing" the Hunter's ideas, and keeping the Hunter on track and on task. If both are committed to the process and can recognize the strengths and weaknesses of the other, such a partnership or team can be very successful.

Unfortunately, Hunters are often drawn to other Hunters, rather than to Farmers. Two Hunters will understand each other, and, sharing mutual energy, can work each other up into an impulsive frenzy with a new idea or concept. However, without a Farmer to provide the slow, steady, supportive personality necessary to keep projects on track, Hunter/Hunter partnerships often spin out of control, crashing and burning in spectacular and often very public blazes.

Partnerships of two or more Farmers, on the other hand, sometimes seem to get nowhere. The entrepreneurial landscape is littered with companies which got started, but never had the necessary spark to move ahead and ultimately died out. Both parties were too careful, methodical, and evaluative. Everything was well thought out—but nothing ever "caught fire."

❖ **Postpone every decision by a day.** If a Hunter doesn't have a nearby Farmer to slow and balance the Hunter's impulsiveness, it's possible to create an "internal Farmer" by adopting a simple technique: wait a day. The guidelines of Alcoholics Anonymous and other 12-step types of programs seem custom-made for dysfunctional Hunters, and one of the first and fundamental techniques a recovering alcoholic or substance abuser learns is to wait—for just one day. That's about how long it takes for a "weak impulse" to fade away, and if a Hunter gets in the habit of simply postponing

for a day that final snap decision, many of those decisions will melt into the fabric of time.

In other words: learn to procrastinate.

It's curious that this natural characteristic of the
hard-core Farmer—to postpone decisions and procrastinate in the name of "thinking things through"—is one
of the most upsetting things to a Hunter. Nonetheless,
it's a useful trait to cultivate.

Write the idea or decision down, and then wait
until tomorrow to do something about it.

One Hunter tells the story of how, when in college,
he would always place a letter to his then-girlfriend in
the drawer overnight before mailing it. Viewed the next
day, the impulsive thoughts expressed in the letter
often seemed in need of toning down, which mini-
mized the chance of relationship disasters.

❖ **Break jobs into little pieces.** One of the big
complaints that Farmers have about Hunters is that
"they start a million things, but never finish any of
them." This problem derives from impulsivity—the
new project is started on an impulse, then a new
impulse drives the Hunter to abandon it for another
new project. So how can a Hunter achieve the persistence necessary to accomplish anything of importance?

Some years ago, I was at the home of an old friend
who's a successful novelist—and a classic Hunter. This
fellow had held dozens of jobs in his life, most very
successfully for a short time before he "burned out"
and quit to try something else. He'd been through
several wives and probably twenty apartments and
houses. But, years earlier, he'd started writing and was
now making a good living at it.

I looked at the three-inch-thick stack of paper on
his desk, a manuscript for a new novel ready to go off

to a publisher, and said, "How do you do that? How can you maintain the energy to write 500 pages?"

Expecting to hear something about the wonders of Chinese Ginseng or wheat germ, I was surprised when he said, "Five pages a day."

"What?" I said, amazed by the simplicity of his answer and wondering if he was making a joke.

"It's simple," he said. "If I write five pages a day, at the end of a hundred days, or about three months, I've written a novel. I do my re-write at the rate of fifteen pages a day, so that takes another month. That means I can predictably turn out three novels a year."

"How long does it take you to write five pages?" I asked.

He turned his hand palm-side up, then over again. "It varies. I start writing when I get up in the morning. Sometimes I'm done by 10 a.m. and I can have breakfast and spend the day reading or playing. Sometimes I'm not finished with those five pages until midnight. But I've taught myself to never go to sleep until that day's five pages are finished."

Since that conversation, I've heard many other successful writers, all to some degree Hunters, say much the same thing. Edison and Tesla followed that dictum when producing their world-changing inventions. Many businesspeople use the principle to get large jobs done. "Break a large job into smaller components and then tackle them one at a time," is one of the basic rules that Dale Carnegie put forth, and it's as useful a bit of advice now as it was in 1944, particularly for Hunters.

❖ **Craving** is the other side of the coin of impulsivity. Hunters often describe strong urges and desires, be they for sweets, sex, excitement, drugs, alcohol, success, or toys. Some Farmers hear these descriptions of a Hunter's cravings and simply cannot understand them: the only time they'd experience a desire that strong might be moments before orgasm. Yet many Hunters live with daily cravings that drive them through life, often in self-destructive directions.

The high percentage of Hunters in our prisons attests to the dangerous power of cravings mixed with impulsivity. Particularly as children, Hunters sometimes totally disregard the long-term consequences of their behavior, so strong is the urge to "get" whatever they want or "do it now." This is probably related to the elasticity of time experienced by Hunters—if they have to wait for gratification, it seems like *forever*. To a person who's profoundly affected with the Hunter gene, it often seems as if there simply never will be a future to contemplate, so why worry about the consequences of today's actions? This, of course, can lead to disaster.

In the sales arena, there's an old maxim about how the easiest people to sell something to are other salespeople. It's generally true, and the reason is that sales is a natural profession for a Hunter. And all you have to do to get a Hunter to buy something is to stimulate his desire, his *craving*, for it. Hunters are the original impulse buyers.

Hunters are more likely than Farmers, particularly as adolescents, to engage in risky behavior. They're more likely to try drugs, tobacco, and alcohol—and more likely to become addicted to them. They're more likely to jump out of airplanes, off bridges with bungee cords attached to them, and to hop into bed with somebody they don't know particularly well.

It's almost as if some Hunters have a constant

yearning for something; a yearning that can't ever be satisfied for more than a brief time. They have passionate affairs that burn out rapidly. They're always experimenting with themselves and the world.

The dangers of a Hunter letting his cravings mix with his impulsivity are obvious. Having discussed how to get control of impulsivity, here are the three techniques a Hunter can use to redirect his or her cravings:

❖ **Wait for it to pass.** Some decisions are just plain wrong, yet the craving is strong. However, if they resist the craving—be it for food, sex, or a new toy (like a cellular phone or a new car)—for even a few hours it'll often pass.

❖ **Redirect the craving.** Freud talked about the "free-floating libido." While we think that the object of our love is the only person we'll ever love, in fact it's love itself that we're experiencing and the person on the other end of it is only a vehicle for us to experience our own love. In other words, the desire is internal, not external, and can be attached to something other than the one thing to which we think it's attached. So, for the Hunter with more than one goal (and often Hunters have multiple "irons in the fire," or goals that they're trying to achieve at the same time), simply concentrating on Item B, when the craving for Item A comes along, will give time to diminish the craving for Item A to the point where it can be ignored long enough for it to go away.

In other words, if fighting a craving is difficult for you, don't say no to it, but, instead, say yes to something else for a while. Often the original desire will pass.

—

Chapter Eight

How to Work with a Hunter: Practical Advice for Managers, Parents, and Teachers

Great works are performed, not by strength, but by perseverance. He that shall walk, with vigor, three hours a day will pass, in seven years, a space equal to the circumference of the globe. —Samuel Johnson

IN THE WORKPLACE— MANAGING A HUNTER

I once served as a consultant to a large chain of retail stores and, when discussing their employment policies, was told by an executive, "We look at a person's job history. If they're job hoppers, we don't consider them for employment. We avoid people who can't stay with a job for at least four years."

This perspective is common sense for a retailer who recognizes that training staff is a significant expense—and has no use for the skills that a Hunter can bring to the workplace. A store clerk is not expected to do much more than ring up a sale. Creativity and personal initiative are unnecessary.

On the other hand, when I was conducting training for a large travel agency in New York State, the owner told me, "We expect our outside salespeople to last about two years; that seems to be about the average. While our inside people, the reservations agents, usually stay with us for five years or more, for some reason, the outside salespeople go off to other things in about two years."

Oddly, she saw it less as a problem and more as a basic reality. Certainly difficulties were involved in bringing new salespeople on board, training them, and getting them up to speed. But good salespeople were so solidly capable of repaying that learning curve that this business owner willingly paid the price every two years or so.

These two examples illustrate the importance of matching job function with personality type. Farmers make excellent store clerks; Hunters are better salespeople. And while a Hunter may not stick with a job for his or her entire career, an employer can often wring enough job performance out of that Hunter to easily pay for the learning curve of the replacement Hunter. (Many sales-driven organizations base their business plans on the assumption that there will be high turnover among their salespeople.)

Hunters do, however, need an extraordinary amount of structure in the workplace. Here are a few quick guidelines:

❖ **Define expectations in measurable, single, short-term goals.** This helps Hunters break large jobs into smaller parts and bring their extraordinary powers of short-term focus to bear on them. Rather than saying, for example, "We want to increase sales by 10 percent this month," try saying, "I want you to be making ten cold-calls a day." The more specific, definable, and measurable the goals, the more likely they'll be reached. And, when possible, give them only one priority at a time.

❖ **Build in daily evaluation systems.** Since their time sense is quite different from Farmers, a day is a long time in the life of a Hunter. By meeting with a Hunter daily, or having a Hunter fill out a daily report, the odds are greatly increased that the Hunter will meet or exceed his or her goals.

❖ **Offer short-term, rather than long-term, rewards.** While a Farmer may be able to visualize the vacation she'll earn if her two-year performance exceeds her goals, this payoff is too distant for a Hunter. A $100 bill pinned to the wall if he meets his goal this week is much more likely to motivate a Hunter.

This is not to say that long-term goals and rewards shouldn't be defined or offered to Hunters: they should. But history shows us that short-term rewards and measurable short-term results are far more relevant to a Hunter than their long-term counterparts.

❖ **Create systems-driven, rather than people-driven, work, home and school environments.** Hunters are often chronically disorganized, and a properly structured work system will help keep them in line and on task. Such systems should include daily definitions of job, performance, goals, and self-measurements. For example, for a salesperson, you may require a form which asks, on a daily basis, how many cold-calls were made, how many follow-up calls, how many client service calls. The salesperson fills it in as the day goes along, keeping him- or herself on track. And the "template," which defines the sales job, might say, "You're expected to make at least ten cold-calls every day to try to bring in new clients. Each existing client is to be called once a month."

IN SCHOOL AND AT HOME—TEACHING OR PARENTING A HUNTER

Over the years, our school systems have experimented with numerous programs to meet the needs of "special" children. Some addressed the boredom and need for stimulation often experienced by very bright students. Others looked at ways to motivate the seemingly unmotivated child. Still others sought to compensate for the behavioral disruptions of "problem" children.

To date, though, few programs outside of the mainstream classroom model have attempted to deal with the ADD or Hunter-type child. Since ADD has been viewed as a "disorder" or a "disease," its logical treatment has been drugs or medicine.

Therefore, millions of Hunter children are sitting today in Farmer classrooms—on drugs. (Testimony before the US Senate in 1975 put the number of children taking medication for hyperactivity at over 2 million. In the nearly two decades since that time, most experts believe the number has more than doubled, and a fourfold increase is not inconceivable.)

Because many Hunter-type children are also above average in intelligence, they're often able to fake it, making their way through school paying attention only 20 to 30 percent of the time. Sometimes their ADD isn't noticed or diagnosed until they reach junior or senior high school, where the increased demands for organization and persistence exceed their ability to use their usual coping strategies or outfox the system with their raw intelligence.

A variety of systems can easily be implemented to keep Hunters on task. More importantly, special educational programs targeted toward "bright" children shouldn't be unavailable to ADD Hunters simply because they haven't succeeded in Farmer-oriented classrooms. Because many of the "gifted children's" special classes are project- and experience-based, providing more opportunities for creativity or shorter "bites" of information, special classes may be a place where a failing Hunter could excel.

Here are a few other simple systems which will help Hunter children succeed in school:

❖ **Create a weekly performance template and check it daily.** Each Hunter child should have a single weekly grid with classes on the vertical axis and the days of the week on the horizontal axis. Each day, the child's performance (both positive and negative— turned in his or her homework or failed to turn in the homework, etc.) is charted both by teacher *and* parent. Creating a larger-than-the-child system will help keep ADD children on task and on time.

❖ **Encourage special projects for extra credit.** Hunter kids do well with special projects (for reasons already cited). These give them an opportunity to learn in a mode that's appropriate to their disposition, and provide them a chance to maintain high grade point averages even if they're not always consistent in doing their "boring" homework.

❖ **Label them as Hunters or Lookouts, not as "Disordered."** Labels are powerful things. They create for us paradigms through which we see ourselves, the world, and our place in it. For children (who struggle far more with issues of "who am I?" and "where do I fit in?" than do adults), applying a label that says "you have a deficit and a disorder" may be more destructive than useful.

This book puts forth a new model to view ADD, a new paradigm which is not pejorative and won't diminish a child's view of his or her own self-worth and potential.

To say, "You have a disorder," is to tell a child that he or she has less potential than others; that he or she will be trouble or cause problems; that he or she has an excuse on which to blame his or her failures. None of these messages are constructive, particularly since ADD can be so easily characterized in a way that leaves self-esteem intact: as a collection of adaptive mechanisms and personality traits that are more suited to some societies and tasks than others.

To tell a child that his or her personality is well adapted to some areas, and that he or she may experience difficulties in others—and to offer ways around those difficulties—usually enhances self-esteem. There's often something very positive about the Hunters in our society, as this book points out. The positive aspects of their uniqueness should therefore be stressed to Hunter children so they can nurture and develop personality traits which may make them successful in later life.

❖ **Reconsider our programs for "gifted" children.** In an Atlanta-area school, there is a program for the "smart" kids called Target. In the Target program, the children's work is more project-oriented than classroom-oriented. They take field trips. They do experiments to learn the principles they're studying. The program emphasizes *doing* rather than simply sitting in a chair and *listening*.

It's a perfect model for Hunter/ADD children.

The irony of the situation is that there are a number of very bright Hunter children who can't get into the Target program, because the criterion for entrance is grades. And their grades, in the "normal" Farmer classroom system, generally aren't good.

A double irony is that some of the good Farmer children who excel in a normal classroom end up struggling in the Target program. They aren't "wired" for experience-based learning. They work best in the Farmer-style classroom where they were doing so well. The simple truth is that different people learn differently.

So the Farmers who excel in the Farmer classrooms get put into the Hunter classroom, whereas the Hunters can't get into the Hunter Target program because they aren't successful in the Farmer classroom.

The solution, of course, is to determine a child's appropriateness for experience-based learning situations by considering *how they learn*, not how well they're currently doing academically. Children who learn well in a traditional classroom situation should remain there. Children who need a high level of stimulation, smaller classes, and an experience-based learning environment should be placed in programs targeted to those styles of learning.

❖ **Think twice about medication, but don't discard it as an option.** Medicating ADD Hunter children is very problematic. There's the issue of the mixed message it sends to those people who are most at risk to be substance abusers in later life.

And there is a very real and legitimate concern

about the long-term side effects of the drugs themselves. All drugs used to treat ADD modify the levels of neurotransmitters in the brain, particularly serotonin and dopamine. There is some evidence (cited in the chapter *Hunters on Drugs*) that these different levels of neurotransmitters may trigger a compensating mechanism whereby the brain grows new neuroreceptors, or adjusts its own level of neurotransmitter production to compensate against the drug-induced "abnormal" levels.

Since later-life conditions such as Parkinson's and Alzheimer's disease are neurotransmitter-level-related, some of the medical literature expresses concern that children who are medicated for ADD may be more at-risk for such conditions in later life. Additional concerns exist over rebound effect, addiction, and cravings for other drugs that long-term use of stimulants or tranquilizers may cause.

On the other hand, in the absence of support systems or special classrooms to meet his or her special needs, not medicating an ADD Hunter child may also lead to problems. Without extraordinary compensatory intelligence, many of these children will simply fail to make it through high school, often being a disruptive element in the school until they finally give up and drop out. Viewed in this context, the relatively unknown long-term risks of drug therapy may be more than offset by the short-term benefits of improved classroom performance.

It's interesting to note that parents report many children who were diagnosed as ADD and failed in the public schools sometimes excel in private schools. Smaller classrooms, more individual attention with specific goal-setting, project-based learning, and other methods discussed earlier are quite common in private elementary and secondary schools.

These systems have demonstrated that ADD/Hunter children don't necessarily need drugs to succeed in school.

The unfortunate reality, though, is that most public schools don't have the resources to replicate the private school environment for ADD Hunter children, although as more information about the scope of the "ADD problem" filters down to the taxpaying general public, to parents, and through school administrations, this situation may change. The cost to schools and, particularly, to society (through lost potential as ADD Hunter children fail in school, and then in life), is greater if nothing is done than if proactive programs were instituted.

A new view of ADD, as a natural adaptive trait

Trait as it appears in the "Disorder" view	How it appears in the "Hunter" view: they're...	Opposite "Farmer" trait: they're...
Distractable.	Constantly monitoring their environment.	Not easily distracted from the task at hand.
Attention span is short, but can become intensely focused for long periods of time.	Able to throw themselves into the chase on a moment's notice.	Able to sustain a steady, dependable effort.
Poor planner: disorganized and impulsive (makes snap decisions).	Flexible; ready to change strategy quickly.	Organized, purposeful. They have a long term strategy and they stick to it.
Distorted sense of time: unaware of how long it will take to do something.	Tireless: capable of sustained drives, but only when "hot on the trail" of some goal.	Conscious of time and timing. They get things done in time, pace themselves, have good "staying power."
Impatient.	Results oriented. Acutely aware of whether the goal is getting closer *now*.	Patient. Aware that good things take time; willing to wait.
Doesn't convert words into concepts adeptly, and vice versa. May or may not have a reading disability.	Visual/concrete thinker, clearly seeing a tangible goal even if there are no words for it.	Much better able to seek goals that aren't easy to see at the moment.
Has difficulty following directions.	Independent.	Team player.
Daydreamer.	Bored by mundane tasks; enjoy new ideas, excitement, "the hunt," being hot on the trail.	Focused. Good at follow-through, tending to details, "taking care of business."
Acts without considering consequences.	Willing and able to take risks and face danger.	Careful, "look before you leap."
Lacking in the social graces.	"No time for niceties when there are decisions to be made!"	Nurturing; creates and supports community values; attuned to whether something will last.

Attention Deficit Disorder: A Different Perception, by Thom Hartmann

Chapter Nine

—

Creativity and ADD: A Brilliant and Flexible Mind

The genius of poetry must work out its own salvation in a man; it cannot be matured by law and precept, but by sensation and watchfulness in itself. That which is creative must create itself.

In "Endymion," I leaped headlong into the sea, and thereby have become better acquainted with the soundings, the quicksands, and the rocks, than if I had stayed upon the green shore, and piped a silly pipe, and took tea and comfortable advice.

—John Keats (Letter to James Hessey, October 9, 1818)

Many teachers, psychiatrists, psychologists, and others who work with ADD children and adults have observed a correlation between creativity and ADD.

Experts define the following personality characteristics as most necessary for creativity:

❖ **The willingness to engage in risk-taking.** Daring to step out into unknown territory is almost by definition a creative effort. Picasso, Dali, Warhol, Salinger, Hemingway, and Poe all struck out in profoundly new and original directions—and were first criticized for their efforts. It's a risk to be original, to try something new. Yet risk-taking is essential to the creative process, and is one of the classic characteristics of the Hunter.

❖ **Intrinsic motivation.** Creative people, while often not motivated by extrinsic factors such as a teacher's expectations or a job's demands, usually have powerful intrinsic motivation. When they're "on a job" that's important to them personally, they're tenacious and unyielding. Parents of ADD children often report the apparent incongruity between their ADD child's apparent inability to stick to his homework for more than fifteen minutes, and his ability to easily spend two hours practicing his guitar, absorbed in a novel, or rebuilding his motorcycle.

❖ **Independent belief in one's own goals.** Creative people, often in the face of derision and obstacles (look at Sartre or Picasso, both ridiculed for their early ideas), believe in their own ideas and abilities. When allowed to pursue those things which they find interesting (their intrinsic motivations), they can be tenacious for years at a time, often producing brilliant work.

❖ **Tolerance for ambiguity.** While Farmers generally prefer things to be ordered and structured, and think in a linear, step-by-step fashion, creative Hunters often have a high tolerance for ambiguity. Because their attention wanders easily, they can often see a situation from several directions, noticing facets or solutions which may not have been obvious to "normal" people. Einstein, who flunked out of school because "his attention wandered off," often pointed out that the theory of relativity didn't come to him as the result of tedious mathematical equations. Rather, the theory was a flash of insight that struck when he was considering the apparently ambiguous nature of the various natural forces. He pointed out that "The whole of science is nothing more than a refinement of everyday thinking" (*Physics and Reality*, 1936). Similarly, Carl Jung, when talking about the ability of creative people to let their minds wander among seemingly ambiguous paths, said, "Without this playing with fantasy, no creative work has ever yet come to birth. The debt we owe to the play of imagination is incalculable" (Psychological Types, 1923).

❖**Willingness to overcome obstacles.** Creative people are often described as those who "when given a lemon, make lemonade." Thousands of businesses and inventions originated with this ability of creative people, often after dozens of different tries. There's an old model of "horizontal" and "vertical" problem-solving: When a person who's a vertical problem-solver comes to a door that's stuck or locked, he will push harder and harder, banging on it, knocking on it, and, ultimately, kicking it in. Conversely, a horizontal problem solver would look for other ways to enter the house, trying windows or other doors. While this is a simplistic view of different problem-solving methods, it does demonstrate the difference between "linear" and "random" ways of viewing the world. Creative individuals more often tend to fall into the latter category. They're usually the ones who devise new ways to do old tasks or to overcome old problems.

❖**Insight skills.** Creative people can make links between seemingly unrelated events in the past, to develop new solutions for current problems. This apparently relates to the ability to think in more random, rather than linear, ways—one of the cardinal characteristics of the typical ADD thought processes.

❖ **The ability to redefine a problem.** Rather than thinking of a problem in the same fashion, creative people often reframe it entirely. This enables them to find within the problem itself the seeds of a solution. Often, they discover that what was viewed as a problem in the past is, in fact, a solution to something else altogether. (The notion of viewing ADD as a Hunter trait might be considered an example of this "reframing" process.)

NURTURING CREATIVITY IN THE HUNTER

When you look through this list of creative characteristics, it reads almost like a recompilation of the American Psychological Association's assessment criteria for diagnosing ADHD. And, reviewing the biographies of some of history's most creative individuals (see the chapter *Hunters Who Have Changed the World*), we discover that they have much in common with ADD Hunters, and, in fact, were most likely people who were "afflicted" with ADD.

A creative Hunter adult describes the experience this way: "The Hunter trait of a constantly shifting point of view is a fabulous asset here. It's what lets you see unexpected things where others see only the obvious. It's like looking for one elusive piece of a jigsaw puzzle, picking something up, and discovering you don't have what you sought but you found something even better instead—it fits somewhere unexpected."

Unfortunately, the risk-taking so necessary to creativity is often pummeled out of our children in school.

Robert J. Sternberg, the author of numerous books and articles on the creative process, points out that risk-taking is often discouraged, or even punished, in a school situation.

Sternberg suggests that our schools, which are largely staffed by earnest non-risk-takers and Farmers, are sometimes unintentionally organized in such a fashion as to discourage both creative people and the learning of creative skills. Similarly, many jobs demand that people not innovate. There are risks in coming up with something new which may not work, so risk-taking is generally frowned upon in corporate America. These anti-creative models are also, probably not by coincidence, anti-ADD/anti-Hunter models.

An educational model that's more experience-based will better preserve and nurture the creativity of the Hunter personality. This is not to suggest that the basics of education can or should be ignored; instead, we should consider establishing public-school class-rooms and systems which encourage activities which will bring out the creativity that's wired into the brains of so many Hunter children.

In the workplace, Hunters may want to consider career or position changes into areas where creativity is encouraged, rather than punished. In my years as an entrepreneur in the advertising and marketing indus-try, I've noticed a very high percentage of Hunters who are drawn to that business.

Hewlett Packard was famous in the 1960s for its workplace model that encouraged engineers to pur-sue areas of independent research, following their own "intrinsic motivations." In *In Search of Excellence*, Tom Peters points out that Hewlett Packard had a policy of "open lab stock," actually encouraging engineers to take things home for their own personal use and experimentation. Two of their engineers, Steve Jobs and Steven Wozniak, came up with an idea for a computer which Hewlett Packard rejected, which Jobs and Wozniak built in their garage: it was the first Apple computer. Bell Labs, too, has historically offered their engineers a similar wide latitude in pursuing creative impulses. The transistor, the integrated circuit, and superconductivity are the result, revolutionizing our world.

An interesting footnote to this discussion about creativity and the Hunter personality: I've spoken with numerous ADD-diagnosed writers, artists, and public speakers about their experience with Ritalin and other anti-ADD drugs. Many report that, while their lives become more organized and their workdays easier when taking the drugs, their creativity seems to dry up. One novelist told me that he uses Ritalin when doing the tedious work of proofreading, but drinks coffee instead when he's writing. "Coffee lends itself to flights of fancy; it seems to make me even more ADD, which allows my wandering mind to explore new ideas, to free-associate. Ritalin brings me to a single point of concentration, which is useless when I'm trying to find that random spark of inspiration about how my character is going to extricate himself from a snake pit in India, or escape a horde of Mongols."

A professional speaker told me, "I made the mistake once of taking Ritalin before giving a three-hour speech to a group of about 100 editors in Washington, DC. Normally when speaking, I'm thinking ahead about what I'm going to say next, formulating concepts into pictures in my mind, dropping in examples before I say them, and continually scanning the audience for cues that my words are either boring or exciting them. But with the Ritalin in my bloodstream, I found myself having to refer back to my notes for that speech—something I haven't done in years. It was a painful and embarrassing experience, and convinced me that Hunters make great public speakers, whereas Farmers, while probably well-organized in their material and presentations, are often boring to an audience because they're not continually scanning their environment."

A writer in the *New York Times Magazine*, describing his diagnosis at age thirty of ADD and subsequent successes with Ritalin, also commented on how much he enjoyed those days when he didn't take his medication. He found that the Ritalin, while smoothing out his emotional swings, stabilizing his time-sense, and giving him the ability to concentrate on his work, also took away a bit of his spontaneity, humor, and sense of the absurd, which he enjoyed.

Reflecting on the dozens of successful public speakers, actors, magicians, other performers, and writers I've worked with and known over the years, I'd guess that many, many of them are ADD adults*.

---

* One Hunter adult suggested, as a title for this book, "I'm not inattentive, you're just boring."

Chapter Ten

Hunters on Drugs

Surely this is the stuff heaven is made of.
— Ralph Waldo Emerson (describing nitrous oxide)

Could it be that drugs are the "cure" for attention deficit disorder?

Sir Arthur Conan Doyle's famous novel *The Sign of the Four* opens with a theme that any fan of Sherlock Holmes will recognize:

> Sherlock Holmes took his bottle from the corner of the mantelpiece and his hypodermic syringe from its neat morocco case. With his long, white, nervous fingers he adjusted the delicate needle, and rolled back his left shirt-cuff. For some little time his eyes rested thoughtfully upon the sinewy forearm and wrist, all dotted and scarred with innumerable puncture-marks. Finally he thrust the sharp point home, pressed down the tiny piston, and sunk back into the velvet-lined armchair with a long sigh of satisfaction....
>
> "Which is it today?" I asked. "Morphine or cocaine?"

He raised his eyes languidly from the old black-letter volume which he had opened. "It is cocaine," he said; "a seven percent solution. Would you care to try it?"

"No, indeed," I answered, brusquely. "My constitution has not got over the Afghan campaign yet. I cannot afford to throw any extra strain upon it."

He smiled at my vehemence. "Perhaps you are right, Watson," he said. "I suppose that its influence is physically a bad one. I find it, however, so transcendently stimulating and clarifying to the mind that its secondary action is a matter of small moment."

When Watson continued his protest at Holmes' use of cocaine, Holmes replied a few paragraphs later:

"My mind," he said, "rebels at stagnation. Give me problems, give me work, give me the most abstruse cryptogram, or the most intricate analysis, and I am in my own proper atmosphere, I can dispense then with artificial stimulants. But I abhor the dull routine of existence. I crave for mental exaltation. That is why I have chosen my own particular profession...."

(If there's a literary archetype of the ADD Hunter, it's certainly Sherlock Holmes, who notices everything around him, and leaps from thought to thought with the grace of a gazelle.)

I recently visited an adult ADD support group meeting in a major American city. The speaker, a psychiatrist, asked for a show of hands:

"How many of you have been diagnosed as ADD?" About half the room raised their hands. (There were many newcomers that night, the result of a recent television show about ADD and this particular support group.)

"How many of you are on medication for your ADD?" Virtually all the adults who had raised their hands for the "diagnosed" question raised their hands.

"How many of you, at one time or another in your life, have self-medicated?" More than four-fifths of the room raised their hands. Those who didn't looked around self-consciously, and the thought struck me that most likely they had, but were afraid to admit it.

The psychiatrist continued with the story of how he, himself, had survived medical school. "Black Beauties (an illegal form of 'street amphetamine') were what got me through," he said. "They heightened my ability to concentrate and study, and many of my friends in medical school were taking them, too."

DRUG USE IN HISTORY

Taking drugs to make it through a difficult job requiring great concentration is nothing new: during "Operation Desert Storm," the United Nations operation against Iraq in 1991, a news report by Cable News Network revealed that United States Air Force fighter and bomber pilots routinely took amphetamines to keep them alert during their flights and have been since before World War II. (The practice was officially discontinued in April 1992, apparently because of the CNN report and other adverse publicity in the midst of the administration's "war on drugs.") Records also show that John F. Kennedy often took methamphetamine, a drug similar to Ritalin, while he was President of the United States.

Sigmund Freud, for several years during his practice of psychology, was of the opinion that cocaine was a wonder drug which would unlock the doors of the unconscious and restore "functional ability" to "dysfunctional" people. Freud, who himself used cocaine, even composed a poem in praise of the drug, and suggested that *every* patient in therapy should be given cocaine. It wasn't until years later, when some of his patients began to overdose on the drug or show signs of drug abuse and addiction, that he reversed his position and suggested that drugs in therapy should be administered carefully, on a case-by-case basis.

Here in America, an Atlanta, Georgia, pharmacist named John Pemberton came up with a formula for a "cure-all" tonic in 1886. He claimed it would cure depression, lack of concentration, headaches, and a host of minor ailments. The tonic formula was purchased five years later by Asa Candler, another pharmacist, and added to carbonated water, producing a soda-fountain drink. By the turn of the century, Coca-Cola could be purchased in virtually every city in America, Hawaii, Canada, and Mexico, and contained as its main active ingredient the substance after which it was named: cocaine. It wasn't until the second decade of the twentieth century that the cocaine was replaced by another powerful stimulant drug, caffeine.

Drug use has been with us for a long, long time. Evidence of the use of fermentation-produced alcohol is well documented in the Bible, and some archaeologists claim that early cave men used the drug. Other cultures have chosen opium, coca, tobacco, or marijuana as their drug of choice. Psychiatrist Andrew Weil postulates that the "urge to alter consciousness" is a basic human drive, just like the drives for food, sex, and security, and he points to children's games where kids spin around in circles until they're dizzy, and animals which will seek out fermented fruit or psycho-active plants, as examples of this instinct.

When Dexedrine was first marketed in 1938, its promoter, Dr. Bradley, hailed it as a "miracle mathematics pill" for its ability to help students perform difficult math projects. Nancy Reagan, while making public pronouncements that people should "Just Say No" to drugs, was herself taking psychoactive drugs, albeit with a doctor's prescription. And it was confirmed in 1992 by the White House that President George Bush and Secretary of State James Baker both occasionally used Halcion, a controversial and powerful tranquilizer in the Valium family, most often prescribed as a sleep aid.

Who among us doesn't drink an occasional cup of caffeine-containing coffee, tea, or cola? And anybody who's been to an Alcoholics Anonymous (AA) meeting knows full well that a majority of the attendees are not living drug-free lives: they consume coffee in prodigious quantities, often smoke tobacco, and some are on prescription drugs which include tranquilizers or stimulants. (This is not to minimize the extraordinary benefits of participation in AA, or the incredibly destructive effects of alcohol addiction; clearly it's one of the most dangerous drugs available, and consumption of it by an alcoholic is tantamount to suicide. AA has probably saved more lives, both directly and indirectly, than any other organization in America.)

Given the pervasiveness of drug use in human history, and the way that over-the-counter drugs are promoted on television as quick cures for everything from arthritis to the common cold, it shouldn't surprise anyone that a first response of our culture to the "disorder" of ADD would be to administer drugs.

DRUGS FOR ADD

Stories of Hunter adults who drink ten to sixty cups of coffee a day just to make it through their unpleasant Farmer jobs are standard fare at any meeting of ADD adults or psychiatrists who specialize in ADD. Replacing these massive, and often ineffective, amounts of caffeine with a small dose of Ritalin or Dexedrine often produces an amazing transformation, "curing" the attention deficit disorder so long as the person is on the drug.

It doesn't work for everyone, but it does produce results for many. Wives tell stories of their newly medicated husbands "paying attention to me, really sitting in one place and listening to me for a half hour, for the first time in years." Relationships improve, people are more functional in the workplace, entrepreneurs become managers, children in trouble become good students and view their former trouble-making peers with disdain. Even some alcoholics and drug addicts (most likely, the ADD Hunters among that sub-population), who claim that their initial attraction to alcohol or drugs was to "stop the boredom" or "turn off all the inputs," find that their craving for alcohol and/or drugs drops off dramatically when they begin Ritalin therapy. There's also growing anecdotal evidence that impulse-control problems, such as sexual promiscuity (and possibly even rape, crimes of violence, etc.), are controllable when the ADD person is medicated with Ritalin or other substances routinely prescribed for ADD.

Sitting in the back row of the Adult ADD Support Group, listening to people tell stories about how Ritalin or Dexedrine had saved their lives, made me wonder if I would have heard similar stories from Arthur Conan Doyle, who claimed that cocaine gave him the genius to write the Sherlock Holmes stories. Would a group of Freud's cocaine-taking patients have offered the same reports? Or a ladies' group in the nineteenth century who all imbibed Lydia Pynkham's Tonic, one of the dozens of over-the-counter tonics containing cocaine, opium, or both, that were sold for over 150 years in America, and consumed by such respectable people as senators, presidents, and their wives? Heroin, too, was first introduced to the market as a cough syrup, and was available for years in corner markets and pharmacies without a prescription; many people reported that it cured more than just their coughs, and use of the "elixir" became quite popular among the "educated classes."

So, again, the question: could it be that drugs *are* the "cure" for attention deficit disorder?

Certainly there is a huge body of medical and anecdotal evidence that says "Yes." Ask any teacher: Ritalin is so pervasive in our schools now that it's almost impossible to find a teacher who can't tell Jekyll and Hyde stories about troublesome or troubled children who became "A" or "B" students when they started taking Ritalin.

And when we look at our prison populations, with their huge percentage of ADD adults as inmates, one is forced to wonder how these people would have turned out if they were given access to such medication when they were young. Statistics indicate that ADD is far more a "disease" of middle-class white children than of poor blacks or other minority groups; yet many argue that instead of this representing a genetic difference, this only reflects the difference in access to medical care and diagnostic resources between these two groups.

It's also interesting to note that the vast majority of prisoners have experimented with, used, or abused drugs long-term prior to incarceration. (Many continue to abuse drugs while in prison, but that's another story.) Could these be attempts to self-medicate as a way of "curing" ADD? Might they be attempts to solve a medical "dysfunction," a "malfunctioning of the brain," with the corner pusher playing the role that a psychiatrist would fill for a more affluent person?

DRUG-FREE ALTERNATIVES

Viewed in this context, Ritalin therapy for ADD seems like an appropriate, and possibly even conservative, step. And it may well be, particularly for those Hunters who are stuck in Farmer life-situations and have no way out of them, or whose impulsivity is a threat to themselves or others.

But a different view may say:

1. People use drugs to deal with the difficulty of being a Hunter in a Farmer's society; and,
2. The solution is not to change or increase the frequency of medication, but to find Hunter jobs, school situations, and life situations for these people, and teach them the basic life skills mentioned in previous chapters which can enable them to be successful as *Hunters*.

One particularly poignant moment occurred at an Adult ADD support group meeting I attended when a man who had been on Ritalin for nine months, with dramatic and positive results, stood up and said, "What I'm having to deal with now is my anger. My anger over the fact that I'm forty years old and have wasted my life. If I'd known about ADD when I was in high school, and had had Ritalin then, I may have made it through. I might have graduated from college as an honors student. I might be a successful professional now, instead of somebody who's had ten jobs in twenty years. I feel like my life has been totally wasted, and there's no way I can go back and recover those lost years." He had tears in his eyes as he spoke those words.

The paradigm he presented was: "I've been sick and defective all these years and didn't know why. Now I'm cured by taking Ritalin, but I've wasted all those years when I didn't know what my sickness was." And, of course, he's angry about that wasted time—angry with himself, angry with the doctors who didn't diagnose him, angry with the schools who just called him a troublemaker.

But an alternate paradigm might be: "I've been a Hunter all these years, with a set of skills ideally suited to being an entrepreneur, or a writer, or a detective. Instead, I spent twenty years trying to be a Farmer, in jobs that required an entire day's concentration at one desk on one task, and it was a disaster. I wish I could have realized years ago that I was a Hunter, and enrolled in a Hunter school system, and found Hunter jobs."

Probably the practical reality is somewhere in between the two. I've talked with many non-ADD people who have experimented with drugs, including Ritalin, and found them useful when working on a task or project. It may be, as Dr. Bradley said of Dexedrine in 1938, or Freud first believed of cocaine, that *everybody* would gain some benefit from Ritalin. That's what television tells us about the other stimulant drug so commonly used in our culture: coffee.

But, as the legion of coffee-habituates are so quick

to point out, there's a down side to stimulant drugs. People who have used coffee or cola drinks for years often report severe withdrawal symptoms when they stop using them: headaches, lethargy, constipation, even migraine attacks.

There are several chemicals which control or regulate activity of and in the brain (neurotransmitters) which are affected by taking methylphenidate (Ritalin) and most other stimulants. The principal neurotransmitters are dopamine, norepinephrine, and serotonin, along with the chemicals into which they break down (their metabolites). Increased levels of these three neurotransmitters affect the part of the brain which controls our ability to shift from a focused state to an open state of awareness (the frontal lobes). They also affect the part of the brain which controls our sense of time (the basal ganglia, corpus striatum).

[Note: Nearly everybody, Hunter, Farmer, or in-between, has experienced the fluidity of time in their life. For Hunters, it's an everyday occurrence. For Farmers, it's usually brought on by a crisis, such as a car accident. The flood of adrenaline releases massive amounts of various neurotransmitters, causing time to seem to slow down. Countless eyewitnesses to accidents or violent crimes have reported that events occurred "as if they were in slow-motion."]

While being highly focused and not bored (not having the sense that time is passing slowly) may be desirable in a classroom or office setting, these states of consciousness may not be best if a person were, for example, walking through a forest or driving a car, where attention to many details all around them is important. One ADD adult on Ritalin told me the story of nearly causing an auto accident because he was so focused on the car in front of him while changing lanes that he didn't notice the car beside him. "When I'm not on Ritalin," he said, "I notice everything. I walk through the house and turn off lights, pick up lint, and constantly scan my environment. When I'm on Ritalin, I tend to do one thing at a time, very focused."

Everybody innately has the ability to shift between these two different states of consciousness. Even ADD-diagnosed children and adults are able to focus their attention and speed up their time sense when working on a project that interests them. There's also considerable evidence that people can train themselves to shift between open and focused consciousness. When they accomplish this shift, PET scans show that the levels of chemical activity change in the brain. (Although "extreme Hunters" are most often in the open state, and "extreme Farmers" are most often in the focused state.)

So, the first downside of using drugs to control ADD is that a person begins losing their ability to turn on and off a state of consciousness.

The second downside is more a possibility than a certainty: long-lasting changes in brain chemistry may result from the long-term use of medication.

Chlorpromazine, sold as Thorazine, is a tranquilizer which functionally reduces levels of serotonin in the brain (a dopaminergic antagonist). Years ago it was routinely prescribed for schizophrenia. Unfortunately, it was also extensively used inappropriately to control psychiatric patients, because it made them so passive.

In an article for *The Journal of Orthomolecular Psychiatry* in 1981, I reported on a twelve-year-old boy who was referred to a residential treatment facility of which I was the Executive Director. This child had been in the state mental hospital for two years, and was on Thorazine nearly the entire time. We took him off the drug, but for three years after that he experienced periodic seizures known as tardive dyskinesia.

The tardive dyskinesia seizures were caused by the brain's response to the Thorazine. Sensing that serotonin levels were abnormally low, the brain actually grew new serotonin receptors to try to get more serotonin. When the Thorazine was withdrawn, the brain was overloaded with its own serotonin, and the seizures resulted. (We also learned later that the boy had no mental illness and was of above-average intelligence; he'd been "dumped" in the mental hospital because of abuse in his home and a lack of foster homes. Living without drugs, but with extensive therapy for his ADD and other emotional problems, he graduated from high school with honors.)

The same process has been well-documented in dozens of opiate studies over the past 100 years: people who use narcotics for long periods of time actually become more sensitive to pain, because the body's production of endorphins has been permanently decreased, and/or the number or sensitivity of pain receptors has been increased. Similar permanent changes have been observed in the numbers of receptor sites, or levels of neurotransmitters, in the brains of laboratory animals given marijuana or cocaine for extended periods of time.

Some researchers assert that ADHD is the result of low levels of dopamine in the brain. Ritalin and other stimulants increase dopamine levels, which appears to be how they "cure" ADHD/ADD. If the brain reacts to the increased levels of stimulant-induced dopamine the same way it does to serotonin level changes induced by Thorazine, or endorphin level changes induced by opiates, then the result of long-term use of stimulants would be that, when they were discontinued, the patient would be *more* ADD than before the beginning of the therapy. Normal levels of dopamine would be lower, as a result of having taken the drug, because the brain's "compensating mechanism" would have kicked in to try to get rid of the extra dopamine. It's important to emphasize that, while this effect has been documented with two other major families of drugs, and research indicates long-term and possibly permanent changes in brain chemistry from extended use of cocaine, no studies have been done which document (or refute) the possibility of this happening with Ritalin.

Since dopamine disorders in old age are at the root of Parkinson's disease, and methylphenidate (Ritalin) affects dopamine levels, there has been some concern expressed that use of this drug over years may have negative side effects in old age.

There's also the concern that tolerance to Ritalin and other stimulants may develop, indicating long-term changes in the brain. One group of researchers, using the language of their trade, reported that after a three-week regime with methylphenidate "desensitization of cortisol and prolactin response [namely, suppression] to methylphenidate rechallenge might indicate development of sub-sensitivity of post-synaptic dopamine receptors following long-term dopamine agonistic activity of methylphenidate." (Translation: "Over three weeks people became progressively less sensitive to methylphenidate in their bloodstream, and this may indicate that changes are taking place in the parts of the brain that react to the drug.")

Animal studies have also demonstrated a cross-tolerance between methylphenidate, cocaine, and amphetamines, indicating that all three of these substances affect the brain in similar fashions.

Other side effects to the use of stimulants include increases in blood pressure, weight loss, and occasional hair loss. Fortunately, none of these seem to be particularly widespread or problematic when dosages are carefully controlled. Some experts have expressed concern about methylphenidate affecting the growth of children, but these studies are too new to be considered conclusive; for now the evidence is marginal. Production of Human Growth Hormone (HGH) by the pituitary gland appears to occur mostly during times of sleep, and at these times methylphenidate levels are lowest in the bloodstream.

In the 1980s a group affiliated with the Church of Scientology launched an aggressive campaign against the psychiatric profession's use of Ritalin with children, raising many of these concerns. Psychiatrists refer to that time as the "Ritalin scare," and often dismiss the concerns raised by this group because of the Church of Scientology's well-known disdain for the psychiatric profession.

Neither side of this issue, however, has been demonstrated as a medical certainty. While Ritalin has been in use since the 1950s, has a relatively short half-life in the body, and is considered relatively safe (I recently heard a psychiatrist publicly refer to it as "safer than aspirin"), no long-term well-controlled studies have been done on its affects among people who use it from childhood through adulthood and into old age. Since it's only in the past ten years or so that adult ADD has even been recognized by the psychiatric profession in general, no long-term studies of Ritalin usage among adults have yet been conducted.

On the other hand, there is little evidence that Ritalin poses a serious risk of the problems postulated earlier. Since no controlled studies have been done on either side of the issue, it's difficult to truly assess its risk. Considering how powerful the withdrawal from caffeine, tobacco, and alcohol can be, however, Ritalin may ultimately be viewed as rather benign when compared to these "normal, recreational" drugs of our culture.

The final question, particularly for schoolchildren, is whether Ritalin is an aid to learning, or merely a way of compensating for behavior difficulties which make learning difficult in a school environment.

Certainly, numerous studies show that many children's grades improve when they take Ritalin. But, again, this doesn't prove that Ritalin is helping learning. It may only be compensating for deficiencies in the classroom which otherwise make learning difficult for ADD children.

Some authorities believe that people learn fastest and best when they are constantly shifting between a focused and an open state of awareness—taking in information in focused detail, then free-associating openly with that information and hooking it onto various memory pegs in the brain. If this is true, then Ritalin (or other drugs which tend to lock the brain into a single attentional state) may do little to aid learning, or may even reduce pure learning ability.

On the other hand, how much can a child learn when he's disrupting the class, regardless of his state of awareness? With many children, if the school is incapable of meeting their Hunter-personality needs through an "action-oriented, project-based" curriculum, Ritalin may be the only option to provide a learning opportunity. Again, though, many educators would argue that this is not the failure of the child, nor is it due to a "deficiency" or "disorder" that the child has; it is, instead, the inability of the school to fund and structure programs appropriate to the needs of Hunter children, thus requiring the child be medicated in order to conform to the school's Farmer systems of teaching/learning.

At the institution I directed, and in numerous private schools around the country, it has been repeatedly demonstrated that ADD Hunter children are not incapable of learning. They do, however, often need a different structure than that provided in the typically overcrowded, underfunded classroom of the 1990s. Smaller classes, information presented in segments of twenty to thirty minutes instead of one hour, visual aids, instruction in visualization (teaching auditory processing, as mentioned earlier), enforced "quiet times" when disruption is not allowed while children are doing homework, and lots of hands-on experiential work, can all combine to provide a powerful learning environment for ADD Hunter children, even in the absence of Ritalin or other drugs.

For Hunter adults—who are more self-aware than children and more likely to know when it's appropriate to take, or not to take, a drug—the availability of Ritalin or Dexedrine may well be analogous to the availability of coffee or alcohol. The vast majority of adults self-medicate with coffee and alcohol in order to achieve specific purposes. A Hunter who must function in a Farmer job may find that occasional use of Ritalin is a useful thing. If it doesn't impair his or her performance in other arenas, doesn't produce negative side effects, and can be set aside during times of vacation, weekends, or when such "focused" awareness is not absolutely necessary, it actually may be a useful psychopharmacological tool.

THE "PERIODIC DRUG USE" OPTION

Another option would be to use Ritalin or Norpramin for three to twelve months in order to develop new patterns of behavior, and then to drop the use of the drug, or reduce it drastically. Several ADD adults who tried Ritalin or Norpramin have reported to me, "what a shock it was to think like that—I never knew other people could concentrate that way." Over time, many have successfully taught themselves concentration skills that could be carried over into drug-free intervals.

It is helpful to point out to people on drugs the apparent differences in their pre- and post-drug states of consciousness and concentration. This awareness may help them learn to develop the "Ritalin/Farmer-concentration" behaviors during times when they are not using drugs. An analogy would be the use of training wheels on a bicycle: a child uses them until he or she has learned the skills necessary to ride the bicycle without them. Once those skills become second nature, the training wheels can safely be discarded.

The important step in this process is to help the child (or adult) to identify his or her behavior on medication. This must be followed by a conscious effort to transfer those behaviors to non-medicated periods. This process may provide a useful middle-ground between the two opposing camps of "always medicate" and "never medicate."

Ultimately, the use of drugs is a decision which each individual or parent must make for him- or herself but should never be viewed as the only way for a Hunter to develop Farmer skills.

ALTERNATIVE THERAPIES

Debate about non-pharmaceutical treatments for ADD has recently moved from the "fringe" health-food publications into "mainstream" magazines and newspapers. Articles about herbs, homeopathy, vitamins, and EEG Neurofeedback as methods of treating ADD are appearing in the popular press in increasing numbers. Many people are experimenting with these non-traditional therapies. While none can match Ritalin's substantial body of supporting scientific research, it is nonetheless important to touch on these subjects since their popularity is growing and many Hunters or parents of Hunter children may consider them as a therapeutic option, now or in the future.

❖ Herbal treatments for ADD usually focus on the "nervine" category of herbs—those which contain an active ingredient traditionally regarded as "relaxing" or "healing" to the nervous system. These include skull-cap (Scutelleria lateriflora), valerian (Valeriana officinalis), hops (Humulus lupus), blue cohosh (Caulophyllum thalictroides), black cohosh (Cimicifuga racemosa), chamomile (Anthemis nobilis) and lady's slipper (Cypripedium pubescens). Occasionally, herbalists will recommend stimulant herbs, such as ginger root (Zingiberis officinale) or licorice (Glycyrrhiza glabra) for ADD.

It should be emphasized that herbs contain active ingredients which may be toxic in high doses or have side effects. So far, none have been subjected to the rigorous double-blind, peer-review studies which would demonstrate their viability as a therapy for ADD.

❖ **Homeopathy** presents fewer risks of side effects than herbs, because homeopathic remedies work through the "vital force" or "life essence" of a medication.

Homeopaths maintain that the homeopathic substances, when properly triturated, are invested with a subtle power which science has not yet learned to measure, but which, nonetheless, works. Pointing to the fact that science has yet to produce an explanation for the dual wave/particle nature of electricity, and therefore cannot explain how electricity works, homeopaths suggest that their remedies work with these same types of now-inexplicable subtle energies.

Homeopathic remedies suggested for treatment of ADD include Tarentula hispanica, Nux vomica, Lycopodium, Stramonium, Chamomila, Tuberculinum, and Veratrum album. Of course, these remedies should be administered under the care of a licensed homeopath.

❖ **Vitamins** and nutritional supplements have been the subject of medical claims since 1912 when biochemists Casimir Funk and Frederick G. Hopkins developed the vitamin theory of deficiency disease and named the substances "vital amines."

The food supplement that has generated the most interest in the context of ADD is choline. Choline is one of the few nutrients which can penetrate the blood-brain barrier. It is converted into the neurotransmitter acetylcholine directly in the brain. Several recent studies link high levels of acetylcholine to improved memory function, and imply benefits for attention span.

Choline is available as a nutritional supplement, and is found in highest concentrations in egg yolks, wheat germ, whole grains, legumes, spinach, sweet potatoes, and lecithin.

❖ **EEG Neurofeedback** involves the use of a rather complex machine, which sells for between $10,000 and $30,000. The device is a modified electroencephalogram, which monitors the relative strengths of various brain-waves. By sitting in front of a monitor or computer screen attached to the EEG device, with the EEG electrodes on your head, you can see your brain-waves and, so the theory goes, train your brain to increase levels of the "focused-awareness" brain-waves while decreasing the power of the "distracted-awareness" brain-waves.

EEG Neurofeedback devices are principally used by health care professionals, although there are home-use units now coming onto the market in the under-$3000 price range. Those initial studies which claim that the technology can "train away" many of the deficits associated with ADD behavior indicate that thirty to fifty half-hour to one-hour sessions may be required.

While there is little interest within the traditional scientific community about the efficacy of herbs, vitamins, and homeopathy (some would argue because there's little profit to be made selling them), EEG Neurofeedback machines are currently the subject of several scientific studies. As of this writing the results look promising. If these devices actually are successful at helping people train their brains to behave in a non-ADD-like fashion, the question is then raised: could the training occur without the machine?

When the final verdict is in on EEG Neurofeedback, it may simply be a validation of the meditation and concentration techniques discussed elsewhere in this book.

In summary, given the recent "discovery" of ADD, it's difficult to claim total success for any one therapy. Drugs such as Ritalin, Norpramin, and Dextroamphetamine have their proponents, just as there are people who claim to benefit from herbs, homeopathy, vitamins, diet, meditation, chiropractic or EEG Neurofeedback.

In my opinion it is important to recognize and understand the strengths and weaknesses intrinsic to an inborn Hunter mindset. Knowing this, we can modify our behavior and create new life situations which compensate for or accommodate our "Hunterness."

Chapter Eleven

Can Parents' Smoking Cause Childhood Behavior Problems?

What unknown power governs men? On what feeble causes do their destinies hinge!

Voltaire, Semiramis

The question first popped into my mind as I sat in a pub in rural England with four parents of severely hyperactive ADD children. As the parents each lit their cigarettes, they proceeded to tell me absolute horror stories about how their children had kicked in doors, smashed windows, punched and even stabbed their siblings, and violently attacked their parents and their teachers. These kids were out of control with a ferocity I'd rarely seen among middle-class ADD/ADHD children in the United States.

Why would this be? I wondered. Why did it seem that there was so much more violent childhood behav-

101

ior among the children of England's middle class, as compared with America's?

Sometimes we don't notice what's right in front of us because we're so used to it. I'd heard similar stories from parents all over the UK, in Germany, and, particularly in poorer neighborhoods and on Indian reservations, in the United States.

As my lungs screamed in pain from all the cigarette smoke around me, my mind raced back over the many stories and the parents who'd told them to me. I looked at the smoke in the air, and recalled how many other times parents had sat with a cigarette in their hand and told me about their off-the-wall children.

Could it be?

How many, I wondered, of those parents of the most violent children were smokers? My mind began to race through the list. By my recollection, it seemed as if it were a majority, but then memory is often a highly variable thing. Maybe it was just the pain cigarette smoke causes me that was coloring my perceptions.

But the question persisted: Could there be a relationship between parental smoking and childhood violence?

And, if so, what was the mechanism? Was it that parents who smoke are more likely to come from lower socioeconomic classes, where hitting a child as a form of discipline is more accepted? Or could it be that the children had become addicted to the nicotine in the passive smoke and were acting out a craving or withdrawal when they didn't have it?

Sitting in that pub, these questions raced through my mind. I was beginning to feel restless, my nose and lungs on fire, my heart racing as I inhaled their heart-stimulating drug.

At that time, I knew that nicotine is the most addictive drug currently known to man. It's more addictive than heroin (by one measure it's five times more addictive), more addictive than crack cocaine, and far more addictive than alcohol (as you can see from all the smokers at any AA meeting). Inhaling nicotine in smoke causes it to hit the bloodstream and the brain twice as fast as injecting it, so smokers get a more rapid rush than heroin users (which is why they're often so resistant to using nicotine gum, which eliminates the craving but doesn't give the high because it hits the bloodstream hundreds of times more slowly).

I also knew that nicotine is one of the most powerful drugs we know of to affect the central nervous system (CNS). It's wildly more powerful than amphetamine or Ritalin, for example.

It's such a powerful CNS drug that the tobacco plant produces it as an insecticide to kill predatory bugs. Nicotine is purified from tobacco and used as an insecticide in some countries and it's incredibly effective, leaving virtually any insect in its path twitching and convulsing in massive CNS overload. The main reason it's not more widely used on crops, in fact, is because it's so dangerous to humans: three drops of pure nicotine will kill a full-grown man in less than ten minutes.

Wondering if there may be a connection between childhood behavior and parental smoking, I did a bit of research.

The first article I found was in the July 15, 1992 issue of the American Journal of Medicine (Nicotine and the central nervous system: biobehavioral effects of cigarette smoking). In it, researchers pointed out that nicotine is a neuroregulatory drug, which profoundly adjusts and modifies the state of the entire central nervous system. When nicotine is absorbed (by smoking or inhaling others' smoke), dose-dependent neurotransmitter and neuroendocrine effects occur, including increases in blood levels of norepinephrine and epinephrine (two hormone/neurotransmitters involved in the fight-or-flight response), and brain levels of dopamine (one of the neurotransmitters some researchers think is off-balance in children with ADD) are altered. Other hormones and neurotransmitters that flood the brain as a result of exposure to nicotine include arginine, vasopressin, Beta-endorphin, adrenocorticotropic hormone, and cortisol (the violence-enhancing hormone released when a person is under stress). Several of these neurochemicals are so highly psychoactive that they modify behavior at a limbic brain level in a way which is beyond the conscious control of the individual ... as any smoker who's tried to quit will tell you.

This was an interesting beginning, but I narrowed the search to specifically look for a correlation between bad behavior (not just ADD but disruptive or violent behaviors) and parental smoking.

What I found then was shocking.

It began in 1979, when a national survey was done by Harvard Medical School and the University of Rochester, polling 12,000 young people between the ages of 14 and 22 to determine their smoking and childbearing behaviors. Follow-up interviews were conducted annually, and by 1986 it was found that 2256 children, ranging in age from 4 years to 11 years old, had been produced by this group. At that point, the children of these parents were rated as to their behaviors, and it was found that children of smokers were 40-50%

more likely to be extremely disruptive than children born of or living in the homes of nonsmokers. Researcher Barry Zuckerman published the results of this multi-year, large-population study in the September, 1992 edition of the well-known Child Health Alert publication for physicians.

Interestingly, Zuckerman's epidemiological data found that smoking during pregnancy wasn't nearly as likely to cause extreme behaviors among children as was smoking in the house where the children were living. Passive smoke, according to this study, was a clear candidate for the role of cause for the extreme behaviors of many of these children.

Another report discussing this study, published in the Pediatric Report's Child Health Newsletter in 1992, pointed out that the researchers had been so meticulous as to even determine that there was a dose dependent   correlation between how much nicotine the children inhaled in the home environment and how severe their behavior was. They pointed out that children of mothers who smoked more than a pack of cigarettes a day were twice as likely (that's 100% more likely!) as other mothers to have children with highly disturbed behavior, whereas mothers who smoked less than a pack a day were only 1.4 times as likely to produce these types of children.

At first, reading this, I wondered if it might just be that people who smoke generally (particularly in the USA) are more likely to come from lower income groups. In the upper-middle-class suburbs of Atlanta where I've lived for the past decade, I don't know of a single parent who smokes: it's seen as a sign of low class. In England and the rest of Europe, however, that distinction has not yet hit the masses, and smoking is widely accepted. And in England I also found many, many more highly disruptive children than I've found in America among the children of people showing up for ADD support groups. So I wondered, could it be a class or income issue?

No, was the unequivocal answer of this study's authors. They'd carefully factored out issues of class, income, lifestyle, use of other drugs, and even diet from their study. This was smoking around the kids, and only smoking around the kids, that predicted violent and disruptive behavior.

Since that time, I was amazed to discover, numerous studies have been done which corroborated the conclusions of this early Harvard study. One was published in the prestigious medical journal Pediatrics in 1992. In that study, Weitzman and his colleagues found a clear correlation between how much Mom smoked and how off-the-wall (my term, not theirs) her child was. They wrote that the connection was highly statistically significant, which is researcher jargon for This looks like a very strong connection!!

That study's publication was followed by the publication of another, a year later and also in Pediatrics, this time by David Fergusson and two other scientists. They spent twelve years studying children of mothers in New Zealand who smoked, compared to a carefully selected group of similar class/income/lifestyle non-smokers. In this study of 1,265 children, they methodically removed from consideration other possible causes of (or variables affecting) poor conduct, including gender, ethnicity, family size, maternal age, maternal education, socioeconomic status, standard of living, maternal emotional responsiveness, avoidance of punishment, number of schools attended, life events, changes of parents, parental discord, parental history of drug use, and parental history of criminal offense.

Having pulled out every possible factor which could contribute to a child becoming violent, acting out, or engaging in antisocial behavior, only one factor was left, and it was staring them right in the face. Their research found a clear and obvious association between mothers smoking during pregnancy and both poor conduct and attention deficit disorders (their phrase).

Other studies have corroborated these. They include studies done by Fried & Watkinson (Neurotoxicology & Teratology, 1988), McCartney (Central auditory processing in school-age children prenatally exposed to cigarette smoke, Neurotoxicology & Teratology, 1994), Richardson and Tizabi (Hyperactivity in the offspring of nicotine-treated rats: Role of the mesolimbic and nigostriatal dopaminergic pathways, Pharmacology and Biochemistry of Behavior, 1994), Sexton & Fox (Prenatal exposure to tobacco: Ill effects on cognitive functioning at age three, International Journal of Epidemiology, 1990), Wakschlag & Lahey, et al (Maternal smoking during pregnancy associated with increased risk for conduct disorder in male offspring, manuscript submitted for publication), Weitzman & Gortmaker, et al (Maternal smoking and behavior problems of children, Pediatrics, 1992), Bertolini & Bernardi (Effects of prenatal exposure to cigarette smoke and nicotine on pregnancy, offspring development, and avoidance behavior in rats, Neurobehavorial Toxicology, 1982), Cotton (Smoking cigarettes may do developing fetuses more harm than ingesting cocaine, Journal of the American Medical

Association, 1994), and Fried & Gray (A follow-up study of attentional behavior in 6-year-old children exposed prenatally to cigarettes Neurotoxicology & Teratology, 1992).

These studies not only corroborated the earlier ones, but also showed that this effect could be seen in rats and other animals (which rules out the socioeconomic factors theory). In rats and dogs, researchers have found that passive exposure to smoke alters neurotransmitter functioning (Cotton, 1994; Slotkin, 1992), increases hyperactivity and motor activity (Richardson & Tizabi, 1994), and decreases learning efficiency and ability (Bertolini, et al., 1982). In humans, they showed that nicotine exposure could do profound damage to the cognitive (thinking) abilities of children from birth right through the teenage years, and that the longer and more severe the exposure was, the more visible and serious was the damage. Several of these studies focused specifically on conduct disorders, and the results were consistent: exposure to passive cigarette smoke in the home correlates with violent behavior in children.

The mechanism by which this effect takes place is, at this moment, unknown. It is known, however, that cigarette smoke stimulates at least two different parts of the brain at the same time. It stimulates the production of cortisol, the stress hormone, which leads to large releases of adrenaline, epinephrine, and other rage and fight-or-flight hormones and neurotransmitters, and, in the high doses that a smoker inhales, also stimulates the production of endorphins, the naturally-occurring opiates of the brain which produce the high smokers experience (along with the cortisol stimulation).

But while smokers are getting both parts of their brain stimulated, children inhaling their smoke are only getting enough nicotine to stimulate the cortisol mechanism: the dose isn't high enough to produce endorphins.

This is intuitive knowledge to any smoker ask him how he'd feel if he could only smoke one or two cigarettes a day, instead of the twenty or forty he normally smokes. He'll describe how easily upset, on-edge, irritable, and filled with anxiety he'd feel at such a low dose of nicotine which is the sort of dose his children are receiving as second-hand smoke.

Reading these studies, and many others that I came across in the course of my research, I was amazed that the issue of cigarette smoking around children hadn't gotten more coverage in the popular media. Certainly if a child were exposed to, for example, marijuana smoke at home, there would be considerable concern among the authorities about the child's absorption of THC, the active drug in that plant. And the same would be true of parents who smoked crack cocaine. But nicotine?

Then I remembered my days working as a writer and contributing editor to numerous magazines. Nearly all took hundreds of thousands, sometimes millions, of dollars a year from the tobacco companies in exchange for advertising. Who would bite that hand?

Only medical journals like Pediatrics, which don't carry advertisements for cigarettes....

Chapter Twelve

Halfway to the Stars: How Unrealized ADD Can Limit an Apparently Successful Life

If thou follow thy star, thou canst not fail of a glorious haven.
— Dante Alighieri, *The Divine Comedy* (1310)

Movies and literature are rife with stories of people who overcame seemingly insurmountable odds to arrive at a level of success even the "average" person would hardly consider attainable. Examples include Terry Fox, the one-legged man who ran coast-to-coast to publicize the fight against cancer; Martin Luther King, Jr., the obscure African-American preacher who nonviolently freed a nation from the burden of segregation; Helen Keller, the woman born blind and deaf who wrote inspiring literature and revolutionized the world's view of "handicapped" people; and Pete Gray, the one-armed ball player who played in the major leagues.

Just as these people overcame handicaps to reach their goals, many adult Hunters have also overcome the limitations of their baseline attention spans and succeeded in the world and in society. Some are such geniuses to begin with that, like Thomas Edison, they're able to push through, past, around, or over their short attention spans.

Many, however, would describe themselves as the walking wounded.

They've succeeded, using many of their Hunter talents, but also often *in spite of* their Hunter instincts. Just like with the one-armed athlete, they are confronting a personal obstacle in the world of business or education, yet they're still apparently "successful."

When such individuals, who may to all outward appearances be "normal," read this book (or others) and recognize themselves as an ADD adult, they may seek professional help—and run straight into a wall.

Disorders and dysfunctions, by definition, mean that a person cannot function well—they're somehow impaired. So when a successful person walks into the office of a physician or psychiatrist and says "I think I have attention deficit disorder" (and, particularly, if they're asking for Ritalin or other drugs for it), the response of the physician may be, "You seem successful enough; what could possibly be wrong with you?" The result is that people who are functional may be misdiagnosed as not having ADD.

The irony here is the frequent failure of teachers, parents, employers, and professionals to see the invisible handicap that the ADD person must work around. And many Hunters who have sufficiently high intelligence to develop adaptive coping strategies through the course of their lives are even able to "fool" attention tests (which are largely designed for children), and "test out as normal."

These people have the potential, the talents, and the raw intelligence to reach the stars—but as a Hunter in this Farmer's world, they'll often only get halfway there.

"YOU'RE DOING WELL ENOUGH ALREADY"

At a recent support group meeting for parents of ADD children, several parents stood up to tell stories of children they believed were ADD, but whom physicians wouldn't treat because, "The kid is doing okay in school; what's the problem?"

The problem, in the eyes of these parents, is that their children are capable of doing *extraordinary* work, and "okay" just isn't a true reflection of their child's intelligence, nor a realization of his or her potential. One parent told the story of taking his son from a public school with an average classroom size of thirty-five children, placing him in a private school with a classroom size of sixteen children, and watching his grades go from Cs to As. The child had native intelligence which would qualify him as a genius, but this genius was not being realized or used because his Hunter characteristics got in the way of his learning ability in a Farmer public school setting.

Brad, who graduated from MIT and was, by all appearances, successful in the world with his various business ventures, realized that he was a Hunter and thought that Ritalin might help him become more successful in dealing with detailed projects that required long hours of concentration. When he visited a local psychiatrist, the doctor told him that he didn't show any symptoms of "minimal brain dysfunction," and implied that Brad was just trying to hustle drugs. At Brad's insistence, the psychiatrist performed a battery of attention and memory tests, and Brad scored "average." His success in passing the tests was because he'd trained himself, over the years, in ways to get around his short attention span. Using some of Harry Lorayne's classic memory techniques, Brad would create absurd pictures in his mind, or organize lists of things into specific categories. It gave him an edge on the test, allowing his very poor attention span to test out as average, just as his extremely high IQ occasionally tested out as average when he became bored with tests while in school.

Because psychological and medical professionals are largely trained to look for problems, if a person's life isn't in total disarray, he or she is often dismissed as not being in need of help. This is particularly true if the physician is under pressure to limit patient visits (as in a health maintenance organization or HMO), or is worried about pressure from government authorities for excessively prescribing controlled substances such as Ritalin or Dexedrine.

NEEDLESS LIMITATIONS ARE INDEED A PROBLEM

The Civil Rights and Women's Movements have sensitized most of us to the notion that a person may have tremendous potential, but be prevented from realizing that potential because of subtle impediments built into the fabric of our society. "Glass ceilings" and "invisible barriers" are common phrases used to describe these situations. If not for the efforts of heroic people like Martin Luther King, Jr. and Gloria Steinem, our society of the 1990s would be as blissfully ignorant of the subtle barriers blacks and women face as we were in the 1950s, when the United States government worked so hard to maintain segregation of schools, restaurants, and other public facilities in the face of "growing restiveness among the Negroes."

ADD is just now beginning to be recognized by government and educational agencies as a barrier to success in public school classrooms and the workforce. Treatments, including special educational programs designed for Hunter children, are occasionally now included in the range of services some schools offer. The United States Department of Education is also under increasing pressure to address the issue. (For more information or details, write to: The Assistant Secretary, Office of Special Education and Rehabilitative Services, United States Department of Education, 400 Maryland Avenue SW, Washington, DC 20202-2500.)

Unrealized potential, in addition to producing human casualties, is also a loss to our society. How many of us have met a taxi driver or construction worker or ex-con who's so articulate and well-informed that you ask yourself, "What's this guy doing driving a cab?"

In jobs such as cab-driving or being a cowboy, Hunter skills are actually a benefit. Unfortunately, many of these people, although sensing their own innate potential, gave up on ever trying to reach beyond cab driving because of all the obstacles they encountered. If they could either: a) pair with a Farmer, or, b) learn new coping skills (possibly including medication) specific to their areas of weakness, they might instead end up as brilliant statesmen, trial lawyers, entrepreneurs, consultants, salespeople, or detectives.

An ADD adult discussing this situation with me (the difficulty of diagnosis, the confusion about the condition, the variety of options for treatment, and, most importantly, the unfortunate circumstances of those who are ADD but whose pleas for help are ignored or rebuffed) shared this very articulate perspective on the situation, gleaned from his own experience:

Successful ADD-copers (especially adults) already have a lifetime of experience at outfoxing their own short attention. They've learned to get by, to get things done—even though sometimes it ain't pretty to watch.

Picture, if you will, three people taking the same test. You have to watch a long, boring series of numbers flashing on the screen, and punch a button when a certain number pops up. The idea is that people with an attention problem will drift away, won't notice the number, and will get a low score.

The first subject is a typical, non-ADD adult. As he watches, he just plain notices when the number appears and punches the button.

The second subject is the opposite: a severely ADD person. No matter how hard she tries, she just can't pay attention. Score: low. This person is likely to have all the everyday coping problems that come from being unable to focus your attention.

The third person, though, has ADD but has learned to cope. First, he knows he's being tested, and over the years of schooling, he's learned how to get through tests. (Otherwise he wouldn't have had the good grades to be successful!) So he starts by putting himself in the "test-me" frame of mind.

As the numbers start to go by, he notices his attention drifting away, and catches himself—just like a bike rider who notices he's falling, and jerks himself back upright.

But still, despite his best conscious efforts to pay attention and do well on this test, he still drops off and misses one. What happens? The examiner reaches out and makes a mark on the score sheet—and the distraction instantly "wakes up" the constantly-scanning subject.

Notice the difference here: the first and third people are getting similar scores, but their experience is very different. The first one just does it; the third one is constantly coping with a tendency to "fall over," and is getting a similar score by a very different process.

And to cap it off, after he's told he has no attention problem, person number three mentions to the receptionist that he has to stop at the dry cleaner's two blocks away, then he gets in his car and drives right past it.

So there you have it: the absent-minded professor, the disorderly genius, the mathematical wizard who can't keep his checks from bouncing. Thousands of people who might achieve greatness have settled for just getting by. People with rapid-fire, quick-connect minds that hop readily from subject to subject.

People who have adjusted have the same underlying problem. But we've spun a web of tricks that helps us "stay afloat" from day to day. We may do things in a mad flurry at deadline time; we may be expert at blaming problems on others; we may have self-medicated our brains with caffeine, nicotine, and endless busy rituals. And, behind it all, we may feel complete hopelessness about ever getting our lives under control.

I sincerely hope that healthcare professionals will open their eyes to the traits of this form of attention problem. The signs are easy enough to spot. If treatment programs can reduce all the time and effort devoted to simply coping, and direct it instead to success strategies, vast amounts of human potential will be unlocked. The person who's already made it halfway to the stars just might go all the way....

Chapter Thirteen

A Disorganized Collection of "Hunter in a Farmer's World" Anecdotes

Education is not the filling of a pail but the lighting of a fire.   — W. B. Yeats

Many books about ADD, particularly scholarly tomes, contain a few case histories which purport to give clinical examples of the condition. Rather than boring the many Hunter readers of this book with detailed case histories, this chapter offers a collection of anecdotes, each designed to give a brief glimpse into the worlds of other Hunters. Hunters will recognize many of these stories, and Farmers may get a new insight into the world of their Hunter friends, spouses, and co-workers.

A few of these stories are sad, some are encouraging, and many demonstrate how knowledge of their own instincts can help Hunters cope with life in this largely Farmer's society and culture. Hunters have inherited a frame of mind, a way of responding to the

119

world, which has a very sensible heritage. They are not weak, bad, or inconsiderate people. But being a Hunter without realizing it has disabled many people in their work and relationships, while learning to manage their Hunter tendencies has brought many others back into the functional world.

Some of the following anecdotes are from interviews by the author. Some are the author's distillation of a Hunter's story—a "factual" retelling of what may have been a long or convoluted conversation or quote. Others are from public statements made by Hunters, or are summaries of "on-line" conversations on a computer bulletin board service.

Each illustrates a common facet of the unique Hunter personality.

A million projects started, but none ever finished

"Until I met my second wife, I never finished anything. I didn't finish high school, the apartment was always littered with half-completed woodworking projects, I had a dozen different hobbies, and dropped out of three different vocational schools. I dropped out of my first marriage after a year.

"I could never finish a book, and don't think I've ever read a magazine all the way through in my life. I knew I was smart, but always ended up in dead-end jobs and have never had what 'normal' people might call a career.

"When I married my second wife, she pushed me to complete things, and I resented her terribly for it. I often accused her of being a bitch and a nag, whether she was urging me to stay with my job or pick up my socks. But somehow we stayed together for a few years, and she kept me at the same job, too.

"It wasn't until after I realized I have ADD, and that she and I see the world differently, that I began to finish things and pay attention to details. Now I realize what a pain in the butt I must have been to live with all those years."

Single with children

"I'm a working, single mother. It's damn hard. The house is always a mess. I start to clean up the kitchen, and then get distracted by finding something and go off on some other tangent. Or one of the kids will interrupt me, and it'll totally blow whatever I'm trying to do.

"I sometimes get so angry with my children that I treat them very poorly. I've hit them a few times, I get so angry. All I want is a little peace and quiet, but they're always in my face, always wanting this or that, and it makes it impossible for me to do anything.

"As if my being ADD isn't bad enough, two of my kids have it, too.

"Every night when I go to bed, I pray to God for the strength to not get upset or out of control again the next day. And every day, it seems, I blow it again."

A day in the office, going to the water cooler

"I started out sitting at my desk, knowing that I had to review this contract. There was a sound outside, and I looked up and out the window—there was a minor fender-bender on the street. As I was looking back toward the contract, I noticed my vitamin bottle, and that reminded me that I hadn't taken my vitamin today. I looked for the glass of water I keep on my desk, but the cleaning people must have emptied it and left it in the office break room. So, I got up to go to the break room to get my glass.

"In the break room, I noticed that the water cooler was almost out of water. I went into the storage area to get a new 5-gallon jug, and there noticed that the little red light on the phone system's music-on-hold radio was flickering. I punched up the music-on-hold, and heard that the radio station was fading in and out, so I began to tune the radio into a stronger station.

"At that point, my partner came into the storage room. 'How's the contract coming?' she asked, glaring at me as I fiddled with the radio. 'And why's the door propped open with this water bottle?'

"You know the ironic part? I never did remember to take that vitamin."

Misdiagnosed as manic-depressive, bipolar

"I could just never get a handle on life, it seemed. I fell in love with dozens of men, but nothing ever seemed to last; after a few months I'd lose interest in them. I could fall in love with somebody from across the room—just catch that one particular, long look, and, bang, you know that this is it—for a few weeks.

"Anyhow, when I hit thirty, I started getting really depressed about it. I'd changed jobs a dozen times, been through probably a hundred or more men, and often wondered if I was alcoholic because I drank a lot. I never got plastered drunk, you know, but I was drinking two or three drinks almost every night. Living alone, it got me to sleep.

"So I went to see this psychiatrist, who told me that I was manic-depressive, and gave me lithium. Two days later I fell asleep while driving home from work, and woke up in the hospital. My car had run off the road and into the highway guard rail. Thank God I didn't hit anybody else.

"So they began dropping my dosage, more and more, until I was taking almost nothing at all, and it was still putting me to sleep, and I was still depressed. So he gave me Valium, and then another tranquilizer, Prozac. None of it seemed to help.

"It wasn't until I saw a television show about ADD and realized, 'Hey, that's me!' that I knew what was wrong with me.

"But when I went back to my doctor, he said that only children get ADD, and then it's almost always boys. 'You outgrow it,' he says. 'Women don't get it.'

"So I went through three shrinks before I found one who said, 'Yeah, adults can have ADD, and lots of women have it, too.' That validation, and the new insights, therapies, and strategies that came with it, have completely turned my life around."

The Interrupter

"All my life, my mother called me 'the interrupter.'

"'You constantly interrupt everybody,' she used to say. And it was true.

"What she didn't realize was that I *had* to interrupt them. If I didn't interrupt, by the time they were done with their sentence I would have forgotten what I was going to say. I would have been distracted by something else they were saying, and my mind would have gone onto something else, and I never would have made my point.

"When I got into college, I learned how to take notes. And so now, in business, whenever I have a meeting, I always take notes, so I don't have to interrupt people. I can just look back at my notes, at the things I was thinking about. It's hard to do in a social situation, though. Sometimes, with my girlfriend, I'll take notes when we talk. It helps.

"Other ADD people tell me that they're interrupters, too. Or, if they're shy, that they want to be. That they have these raging conversations going on inside their heads. I guess it's part of ADD, because Farmer people I know tell me that they don't need to interrupt, that they can remember a thought for a few minutes at a time, and they let me finish my sentences."

Just get your wife pregnant; she'll stop bothering you

"Before I was diagnosed as being ADD and started working on that as 'my' problem, my wife and I were having terrible difficulties. She felt like I didn't love her, because I'd forget her birthday, or get up and walk off while she was in the middle of a sentence. 'You never pay attention to me,' she'd always complain. I'd just try to tell her that she was being needy and neurotic, but she'd insist that there was something wrong with me.

"So we went to see this marriage counselor. Explained the whole thing to him. You know what his solution was? 'Get her pregnant,' he said. 'That'll give her something else to focus her attention on, and she won't hassle you so much.'

"She wasn't ready for that one, so we tried another counselor who told us that I was ADD and sent me to a psychiatrist, who gave me Ritalin. Now I actually sit and talk with her, sometimes for more than an hour, which is something I don't think I've ever done with anybody else in my entire life. And our marriage is better than either of us ever thought possible."

Applying new skills to the job

"I had a very good computer-technical-support day today, at a major national magazine.

"I realized on the drive home from San Francisco that I successfully handled this situation differently from my usual response, simply by being aware of my ADD tendencies and how I'm different from the mid-road masses. See, typically, while grokking all the stuff about how a client's system is and isn't working, I'll notice a bazillion things that need to be tweaked, each a simple little change. I make the changes in the little slices of time between steps of the main task.

"But people get unsettled by these changes after I'm gone. So this time I took the changes back out. Result: I changed only what needed to be changed to respond to the customer's reported need. Less to keep track of, less to document, less to debug. Less effort, more results.

"A positive change in my behavior, an increase in my effectiveness, without medication, just by being aware of the Hunter versus Farmer perspectives. See, it *can* be done. Didn't even take effort on my part— just by being aware of it, I saw the situation differently."

I've always felt like a fraud and a phony

"A lot of people in my life have commented on how smart I am, and I'm successful as a saleswoman—very successful. But I had a heck of a time with school, and I could never really memorize things, or understand anything like physics that really required concentration. Although I'd done well until then, I almost flunked out in my senior year of high school. So, I never thought I was as smart as everybody always said I was, because I couldn't handle anything that really required concentrating and intense learning.

"All my life, I've felt like a phony. It wasn't until I

learned that I have ADD that I realized it's possible to be both smart and incapable of concentrating long enough to understand physics ...."

Dancing with the stars (an online transcript)

CompuServe Message: #201867
Date: Sat, Apr 11, 1992 5:26:12 AM
Subject: #201735 – attention deficit disorder
From: Marsha
To: Robert

I, too, have never felt ADD is a disorder. My son has a gift (and my sister). Their minds can go places mine cannot, and I'm envious of that. Unfortunately, all gifts have a price – and theirs is a lack of attention to detail. Small price to pay for being able to dance among the heavens during the course of your day, don't you think?
– *Marsha*

CompuServe Message: #201884
Date: Sat, Apr 11, 1992 7:01:15 AM
Subject: #201867 – attention deficit disorder
From: Robert
To: Marsha

Well, m'dear, *you* may call it dancing among the heavens, and *you* may call it a small price. If that's so, then I can tell ya, heaven has lotsa sharp, pointy things to bump into.

The tough thing, for some kids, must be getting treated as "not right" when science is just now beginning to discover how they actually work. The "bad" news is that these discoveries didn't happen in the nineteenth century. The good news is that these discoveries didn't have to wait for the twenty-first century!

In fact, in the long history of such kids, I'd say the ones born 1975-1995 are in a rare, pivotal position.

They are the first, I'd guess, to have a chance to be viewed in the new way. They're pioneers; their contributions to our knowledge will benefit people forever—especially their own descendants (and, therefore, yours).

Do you feel good to be making a contribution to this, right now? (smile)   —Robert

> CompuServe Message: #202429
> Date: Mon, Apr 13, 1992 6:21:09 AM
> Subject: #201884—attention deficit disorder
> From: Marsha
> To: Robert
> When I said, "dancing among the heavens" I was referring to the ability to grasp abstract (heavenly) concepts. People who have this ability don't realize what a struggle abstractions are for some of us. For example, I was a great math student up until calculus. I made decent grades in calculus, too, but strictly by memorization. I never really understood it—too much abstraction. My son, however, struggles with the routine, "easy" stuff, and finds the abstract concepts instinctual.
>
> I know life is full of sharp points for ADD people—believe me, I know. But I still think, as time passes, we'll come to view this "affliction" as a "side-effect" (if you will) of creative, abstract thought.
>
> And yes, I do think this generation is on the cusp. In fact, I often tell my son it will be *his* generation—the first to make it through school in large numbers—who will truly change things for the next one.
>
>   —Marsha

He's speedy, I'm not ... and we're both ADD

"When my husband was diagnosed as having ADD, I thought, sure, this is it. He's hyperactive. He's always on the go, always doing something new, always looking for a different challenge. It makes sense that he's one of those hyperactive people, those ADD people.

"But then I took the test, and realized that I'm ADD, too. I forget things constantly. I'll drive all the way to the store, only to realize when I get there that I forgot what I was intending to buy. While people are talking, I'm thinking a million miles an hour, about this and that, thoughts that go shooting off in some direction because of something they said. And then, a few minutes later, I realize I'm not paying attention at all.

"I'm not hyperactive, I'm pretty quiet, in fact, but I'm ADD. I never thought it was possible."

The "Dingbat Blonde"

"I'm the blonde they make the jokes about. Except it's not a joke.

"I'm smart and I know I'm smart. But before I realized I was ADD and learned the memory and organization exercises, I always played the dumb blonde role and nobody but me knew I *was* smart.

"Being a dingbat was an easy part for me to play, because I could never concentrate on anything, and it was a socially acceptable stereotype. I'd forget a shopping list with three things on it. I can't tell you how many times I've killed the battery on my car because I left the lights on. Somebody will say something that'll trigger a thought, and, poof, I'm off. And then they say, 'There went Debby. The lights are on, but no one's home.'

"Nobody's calling me a dumb blonde anymore, though. I'm even thinking of getting my hair dyed brunette."

Working around ADD

"Here's a tip (before I forget) to ADDers: constantly

losing things? Eliminate ambiguity. Always put things in one place, or at most one of two.

"My wallet is always either in my right hip pocket or on my dresser.

"My plane tickets, when I travel, are always inside my left coat pocket.

"My keys are always on the kitchen wall hook or in my pocket.

"When I travel (I used to lose things in hotels), everything that comes out of my pockets goes on top of the television. This vastly diminishes my confusion in the mornings!

"My personal life is now organized by a small calendar/phone book. The important thing here is that it's tiny and it doesn't have an ouchy spiral binding, so it lives in my left hip pocket. It's always there.

"With this constant predictability, if something's not where it's supposed to be, I know right away that I have to look for it—there's no chance it might be in a dozen different places."

Suicidal adolescents with ADD

"As a teacher, I can tell you that almost every time I've come across a suicidal adolescent, it's been a very bright, or gifted, or genius child with ADD. They can't handle the dichotomy of knowing that they're brilliant, yet unable to do their schoolwork. And the distortions of time-sense with ADD cause their lows to seem so very painfully low that they get suicidal."

An alcoholic who found relief

"When I was seventeen I finally found something that would turn off the constant grinding of the gears in my brain: alcohol. By the time I was twenty-three, I was a full-blown, down-and-out drunk. I hit bottom, and made it back with the help of God and Alcoholics Anonymous.

"But it wasn't until I was thirty and started on EEG Neurofeedback that the constant chatter in my head, the persistent distractions from every direction, stopped. Then, for the first time, I could smell the flowers. I could experience life. I could actually listen to other people, and understand what they were saying.

"And I have gone from fighting the urge to drink, to no longer having the urge to drink."

Cleaning the desk with my Farmer-wife

"This morning my extremely stable Farmer-partner-wife sat patiently with me and took papers off the huge pile on my desk, one by one, and 'brought them to my attention' by sticking them in my hand. Each was disposed of immediately: filed appropriately, put in the Bills To Pay or Expenses Folder, discarded, and so on. An hour into this I got out my briefcase (for a very good reason of course) and started looking for something important; found something else and remembered I needed to send someone a message about something three weeks old. So I sat down to my computer to send an e-mail ... Alarm! She says 'Am I losing you?'

"We've done this 'hand me each paper' thing a few times in the past but I've always felt terrible about having to be babysat. She's been rather disgusted too, and *really* disgusted when she'd start to 'lose' me. 'Hell,' she thinks, 'if I'm gonna babysit him like this, the *least* he can do is not ignore me! If he's not gonna pay attention, I'm leaving!'

"But this time when she said 'Am I losing you?' I shortened the e-mail, shortened the briefcase task, and sat right back down in the 'next-paper-please' chair.

"The desk is now clear for the first time in months. (There are still other piles to be sorted through, but the desk is clear!)

"What a gift it is to have a Farmer-partner who's willing to assist, and for us both to now understand the differences between Hunters and Farmers."

Chapter Fourteen

The Edison Trait: Hunters Who Have Changed the World

I represent a party which does not yet exist: the party of revolution, civilization.

This party will make the twentieth century.

There will issue from it first the United States of Europe, then the United States of the World.

— On the wall of Victor Hugo's room
when he died in Paris, 1885

Hunters sometimes have difficulty answering the question "What do you do for a living?" It's not that there isn't an answer; it's that there are too many answers. Hunters of above-average or genius intelligence often have resumés which are startling in their diversity and accomplishment, even though they may have struggled to simply finish high school.

Similarly, the stereotype of the "eccentric genius" or "loony, creative type" is often applied to Hunter inventors, artists, writers, and designers. At many ad

133

agencies, the "creative types" are allowed (or even encouraged) to have an eccentric appearance, with flowered shirts, long hair, jeans, etc.

As the chapter on ADD and creativity pointed out, the ability to think innovatively is intrinsically tied to the ability to fall into an open (and therefore distractible) state of consciousness. Conversely, to make use of the "inspirations" gained from such typical Hunter free-association, there must be a compensating burst of focused energy, in order to bring these concepts into reality. Learning to channel these bursts is the challenge of every Hunter.

When Hunters fail in life it is often because their self-image was distorted at an early age when they were labeled as a "problem". Their assets are also neglected if they plug into a job or a segment of society which requires Farmer, rather than Hunter, skills.

But let's look at some successful Hunters in history who have demonstrated tremendous powers of transformation, vitality and dynamic energy, and whose biographies appear to conform to the American Psychiatric Association's DSM criteria of ADHD. While it is impossible for us to reach back to historic figures and ask them to answer the questions which might lead to a medically supportable diagnosis of ADD, their life stories very often give us those answers in a rather overt fashion. Consider the following:

The life of **Thomas Alva Edison** has been an inspiration to Hunter boys for nearly a century. Born in the Midwest before the Civil War, Edison wrote, "I remember I used never to be able to get along at school. I was always at the foot of the class. I used to feel that the teachers did not sympathize with me, and that my father thought I was stupid...."

Edison complained about the distractions of the other children in his school, and the fact that learning was "abstract" and not "real." To be able to actually *do* something, to test a theory or discover a fact through *experience* (he wrote in his diary) "for one instant, was better than learning about something he had never seen for two hours."

Believing her son had potential, Edison's mother took over his schooling. Instead of requiring her son to learn a particular curriculum by rote, she instead encouraged him to explore things he found interesting; he soon became a voracious reader and consumed a huge body of knowledge on a wide variety of subjects.

Edison left home at age twelve and started a long procession of short-lived jobs. The year he was seventeen, he held four different jobs, being fired from each one because of his inattentiveness to the duties or routine of the job. When he was fifteen, he had a job as a railroad signalman during the night, and had to clock in via telegraph every hour. He was fired when his superiors learned that his punctual check-in signal was actually transmitted by a simple invention he'd created from an alarm clock, which would send the Morse Code signal on the hour. That invention led to his developing the first automatic telegraph, and then the first stock ticker, although he held a dozen more jobs before he received $40,000 for his stock ticker, at age twenty-one, and was able to establish a laboratory where he could devote himself to inventing.

Being a classic Hunter, Edison usually worked on many projects at the same time. In the year of 1877, for example, we know that he had more than 40 inventions in process in his laboratory—concurrently. He kept his own hours, often working through the night. When he became bored or saturated with one invention, he would quickly hop to another.

Edison credited his *inability* to stick to one task for a long time as being the power of his creative efforts. He said, "Look, I start here with the intention of going there" (drawing an imaginary line) "in an experiment, say, to increase the speed of the Atlantic cable; but when I have arrived part way in my straight line, I meet with a phenomenon and it leads me off in another direction—to something totally unexpected."

Thomas Edison transformed the twentieth century with his invention of the electric light bulb, the central power generating station, the phonograph, the flexible celluloid film and movie projector, the alkaline storage battery, and the microphone (merely a few among the more than 1,000 major patents he registered before his death in 1931).

Benjamin Franklin flunked out of George Brownell's Academy after only two years of formal education. It was said that he was "slow at doing sums," and he utterly failed in arithmetic; his teacher complained that he would never pay attention to his lessons. He spent two years as an apprentice candlemaker to his father, but his father's frustrations with young Ben were legion: the boy was always slipping off to explore the town, the salt marshes, the incoming ships.

Having demonstrated his Hunter inability to be a scholar in the formal Farmer schools of the day, Franklin went on to become one of the most well-educated (in terms of practical abilities) men in American history. Although he couldn't stick with a single job, Franklin is now celebrated for his accomplishments in *dozens* of roles: he was a printer, moralist, civic leader, essayist, inventor, scientist, diplomat, publisher, statesman, postmaster, candlemaker, mechanic, and philosopher, among others.

His impulsive streak, which was partly responsible for the creation of an independent United States of America, showed itself early when, at age sixteen, he wrote several articles for *The Courant*, a Boston newspaper, making fun of Boston's authorities and society figures. His persistence in writing such articles led to the imprisonment of his brother, James, who published the paper. After running the paper until James got out of jail, Ben left his job with *The Courant*.

Taking a huge risk, a penniless Ben Franklin left for England in 1724, where he soon became a master printer and writer. Two years later, upon returning to Philadelphia, he began publishing his own newspaper, the *Pennsylvania Gazette*, and also started, wrote, edited, designed, printed, and distributed a periodical titled *Poor Richard's Almanack*.

Once these two publishing endeavors were up and running well, Franklin, now bored and looking for a new challenge, created a network of printers throughout the colonies to do the government's printing. During this time he also opened a book shop, then became clerk of the Pennsylvania Assembly, and the first postmaster of Philadelphia.

With his businesses doing well and his income assured, he turned over management of his publishing business, book store, and other endeavors to trusted Farmer-types, and went off in search of other challenges, sustained for more than twenty years by the income from these early startups. He founded the Junto Society, which created one of America's first libraries (1731), Philadelphia's first fire station (1736), the University of Pennsylvania (1749), and—in one year—both an insurance company and a hospital (1751). He also organized Philadelphia's first public works department, supervising the lighting, paving, and cleaning of the streets, and organizing a volunteer militia. In 1763, Franklin took on the job of reorganizing the entire American postal system.

During this time of his "retirement," Franklin also pursued many private interests. He invented the Franklin Stove in 1740, which still heats millions of American homes. In 1752 he proposed that lightning was a form of electricity and, with characteristically impulsive abandon, risked flying a kite in a thunderstorm to prove his thesis. His scientific theories and discoveries made him world famous and, in 1756, he was elected to the Royal Society, which numbers among its members Newton, Einstein, and Hawking. He was inducted into the French Academy of Sciences in 1772. He was the first man to measure the Gulf Stream. He pioneered the science of tracking storm paths (which led to modern predictive meteorology). He designed sailing ships, and invented the bifocal lens for glasses. A man who was thrown out of the third grade, he was granted honorary degrees from St. Andrews (1759) and Oxford (1762).

In 1751, Franklin ran for and was elected to the Pennsylvania Assembly. In 1754, he presented a plan to the Albany Congress for partial self-government of the American colonies. Not content to simply sit back in a legislative mode, Franklin himself led an expedition of military men into the Lehigh Valley, fighting both the French and the Indians and building forts there to protect the frontiersmen.

Franklin's personal life reflected the occasionally reckless streak seen in so many ADD adults. He had an illegitimate son, a wife in Philadelphia, a mistress in London, and there were rumors of several other women who kept his company over the years, particularly during the time he spent in Paris where his nickname was *le Bonhomme Richard.*

At the age of seventy, in 1776, Franklin signed the Declaration of Independence that he'd helped draft. That same year, he also served in the Continental Congress, proposed a new constitution for Pennsylvania, and wrote the Articles of Confederation for the United Colonies, soon to become the United States of America. Ten years later, after returning from France, he became president of Pennsylvania and attended the Constitutional Convention of 1787, where the final draft of our Constitution was written with his help.

Sir Richard Francis Burton, not to be confused with the late Welsh actor and husband of Elizabeth Taylor, is perhaps one of the most fascinating Hunters of recent history.

In his early childhood Burton, born in 1821, was described by those who knew him as a "terror." Once when his mother was taking him through town, at age seven, he broke a shop window to get at a pastry she told him he couldn't have. He regularly terrorized nannies, and was a total failure at school, constantly fighting with the other boys and describing his teacher as "no more fit to be a schoolmaster than the Grand Cham of Tartary."

Eventually, Burton made it through to Oxford University, but then dropped out to purchase a commission in the Bombay Native Infantry in 1843. He was a soldier, for the next five years, in what is now Pakistan.

Following his brief career as a soldier, Burton became a world-famous explorer. He disguised himself as a Muslim, "Sheik Abdullah," and became the first West-erner to ever visit Mecca and Medina for the Haj, the holy Muslim holiday. Had he been revealed as a non-Muslim during this trip, he most surely would have been put to death. Following that success, which was widely reported in England, he made an equally danger-ous foray to the Ethiopian forbidden city of Harar.

His greatest exploration, and the one that thrilled the world of European society, was his 1857 exploration of Tanzania. He became, in 1858, the first white ever to view Lake Tanganyika. Having explored Africa, he later crossed the American continent to Salt Lake City, and then mapped the territory to Panama.

Following this flurry of exploratory success, Bur-ton was named British consul at Fernando Po, off the coast of Nigeria, was the first white to visit Benin (then called Dahomey), and was one of the first whites to ever travel up the Congo River. Later, he served Britain as consul in Damascus, Trieste, and Santos, Brazil.

If his explorations weren't enough to establish Burton's reputation, he also wrote twenty-one books that still remain (his wife burned a number of his manuscripts—perhaps as many as fifty—upon his death), including tales of his travels, books on falconry, and an esoteric tome on swordsmanship (of which he was a master). He was a brilliant linguist, and was the first European to translate the *Tales of the Arabian Nights* from Arabic into English, as well as secretly translating a number of Eastern manuals about sexual positions and perversions. During the times of his writing, his easy distractibility caused him to seek rooms in distant monasteries, mountain retreats, and other places where he could work for days or weeks in total isolation.

Burton had an impulsive streak that nearly killed him several times. He was involved in a number of duels and fights-to-the-death as a result of remarks he made without first thinking through their consequences. Although married, he had numerous mistresses all around the world, and publicly advocated polygamy.

Burton's interests ranged from the rational to the spiritual to the bizarre. He became a world-respected authority on reptiles, mining, and mountain climbing. He wrote extensively about slavery, religion, and odd sexual practices. He was fascinated by different cultures, and brought back from his trips to Africa numerous illustrations which shocked and amazed Western anthropologists.

His biographer, Byron Farwell, pointing out the breadth of Burton's career and his astounding range of interests, called him "one of the rarest personalities ever seen on Earth."

When he died in 1890, Burton had made and lost several fortunes, held dozens of jobs and posts, written at least fifty books, changed the western world's perspective on archaeology and African anthropology, and become one of the most respected—and vilified—men of his day.

Ernest Hemingway struggled to make his way through school, finally graduating from Petoskey, Michigan's Oak Park High in 1917. His unpleasant school experiences, the result of his short attention span and "boredom," convinced him that college would be a wasted effort. He instead took a job as a cub reporter for the *Kansas City Star*. After only seven months on the job, Hemingway became restless and tried to enlist in the U.S. Army so he could fight in World War I. When the Army rejected him because of weak eyesight, his desire to take risks and his craving for stimulation propelled him to join the Red Cross as a volunteer ambulance driver and he was shipped off to Italy.

After a severe injury from shrapnel and a brief recuperation in Milan, Hemingway returned to North America and got a part-time job as a feature writer for the *Toronto Star*. Within a year he tired of that, and moved on to a job in 1920 as a contributing editor of a trade journal in Chicago, where he met and married, in a whirlwind romance, his first wife. They traveled to France on their honeymoon, where Hemingway decided to stay, and arranged to be a "foreign correspondent" for his old employer, the *Toronto Star*. In 1923, Hemingway moved to Toronto (where his son John was born) to try to work a regular job at the Star, but the routine and many distractions of the news office drove him to quit his job and, on an impulse, return to Paris, jobless, where he intended to launch a career as a serious and financially successful writer.

It took four years for Hemingway to reach his goal. His first American publication was a small volume of short stories, *In Our Time*, that was published in 1925 (although two small chapbooks of prose and poetry were published in Paris in 1923 and 1924). By 1927, Hemingway had established his reputation as a writer (and was actually making a living at it). He'd published *The Torrents of Spring*, *The Sun Also Rises*, and *Men Without Women*. He also divorced his first wife that year, and married Pauline Pfeiffer.

Hemingway's ADD-restlessness caught up with him again in 1928. He moved to Key West with Pauline, then began a series of world travels, from dude-ranching in Wyoming, to deep-sea fishing in Cuba, to extensive travels through Europe and Africa, where he enjoyed big-game hunting.

By 1940, his second marriage had disintegrated, and Hemingway, seeking to get away from the constant stream of visitors that distracted him from his work, married his third wife, Martha Gellhorn, and moved to a remote farm outside Havana, Cuba. The next year, they flew to China to report on the Japanese attacks on China. When the United States entered World War II, Hemingway armed his cabin cruiser, "Pilar," and cruised around the Caribbean for the next two years, hunting German submarines.

Just before the Allied invasion of Normandy, a new impulse drove Hemingway to London, where he met Mary Welsh, his fourth wife. He joined the Fourth Infantry Division in the summer and fall of 1944, pursued fleeing Nazi forces during the liberation of Paris, and fought in the Battle of the Bulge.

After the war, Hemingway retired again to Cuba, where he alternated between streaks of brilliant writing and wild drinking in his remote hideaway. So great was his need for solitude in order to concentrate, he often shot at visitors who arrived looking for autographs or wanting to meet the "great writer." On other occasions, if he was drinking instead of writing, he might welcome visitors with open arms and engage in all-night drinking and talking sessions, providing wonderful entertainment with his free-associations and wandering stories of his life. (This is a pattern which several ADD alcoholics have reported to me from their own lives.)

Finally unable to reconcile his impulsiveness, his alcoholism, and his easy distractibility which, compounded by the fame which followed his winning the

Nobel Prize for Literature in 1954, led to severe difficulties in writing, Hemingway followed in his father's footsteps and killed himself in 1960.

Thomas Carlyle, whose quote opens the preface to this book, was born about 200 years ago in Scotland to a sternly Calvinist family of peasants. He was described as a skeptic and an empiricist, and, like many ADD adults, struggled through many different attempts at building a career. He started in law, then went to journalism, the ministry, teaching, and mathematics, before deciding, in 1821, to become a writer. He was forty-two years old when his first published work, *The French Revolution*, brought him out of poverty and into the world of published writers. Many of his works such as *Latter Day Pamphlets* (1850) and *Niagra And After?* (1867) were essentially tirades about modern society— a Farmer society which his Hunter's low threshold for frustration and high distractibility had, in his view, kept him from success. Carlyle's work is alternately described by his biographers as "uneven," "rhetorically audacious," and "full of energy."

(Certainly there are many modern people who are both successful and Hunters. A famous, high-energy comedian and actor is often mentioned in informal discussions of ADD, as is the brilliant founder of a major television network. However, since ADD or ADHD is currently classified as a mental illnesses by the psychiatric profession, it would be uncharitable at best, and risky at worst, to reveal or speculate on the mental state of living persons.)

Chapter Fifteen

—

Baseline States of Consciousness

The secondary imagination...dissolves, diffuses, dissipates, in order to re-create; or where this process is rendered impossible, yet still at all events it struggles to idealize and to unify. It is essentially vital, even as all objects (as objects) are essentially fixed and dead....

The fancy is indeed no other than a mode of memory emancipated from the order of time and space.

—Samuel Taylor Coleridge (*Biographia Literaria*, 1817)

This chapter speculates on the nature of various states of consciousness, how they evolved, and how we can best utilize them. What are the differences between Hunters and Farmers in terms of how they experience the world? How different are their realities? Is one state of consciousness "better" than the other in some global sense, or are they merely "separate but equal"? Might other "variations" of consciousness also be adaptive mechanisms left over from more primitive societies?

145

And might there be an opposite disorder to ADD, where the individual cannot *stop* focusing?

TASK-SWITCHING DEFICIT DISORDER (TSDD)

Many modern microcomputers are capable of doing more than one thing at the same time. On DOS-based personal computers it's called "multi-tasking," whereas on a Macintosh computer it's the difference between the "Finder" and "MultiFinder." It works by causing the computer to perform a few hundred calculations on one job or in one program, then shift to the next job or program and perform a few hundred calculations there. Shifting back and forth between two different programs or jobs, one in "foreground" and the other in "background," the computer seems to actually do two things at the same time.

In actual point of fact, though, the computer is only doing one thing at a time. It just switches from that one thing to another and back again so fast (often in a ten-millionth of a second!) that it seems to be performing parallel tasks.

ADD Hunters often report that they consider the ability to do several things at once as one of their "special skills." Betty is most in her element when she has a job printing from one computer, is performing backup onto another computer, and she's doing design work on a third. She reports getting a special satisfaction from her unique ability to do three things at once, when the other computer-based designers with whom she works must plod along on one job at a time.

Conversely, non-ADD Farmers are often irritated by their Hunter-peers' tendency to go shooting off in new directions in the middle of a conversation. "I was talking and Bill just pulled out a piece of paper and started writing," said John indignantly. "I know he couldn't have been listening to me; he was writing."

Bill, however, is emphatic that he could both write down his idea and listen to John at the same time. He couldn't understand why John would get so upset, just because he didn't "seem focused on the entire conversation, every minute."

While John's perception—that Bill was ignoring him as he was writing—may have been correct, it may also be that John was simply judging Bill, using his own abilities as a reference. John, being solidly a Farmer, couldn't imagine trying to do two things at once, because neither would get done well! But to Bill it just seemed normal for people to pay attention to two things at the same time.

Perhaps Bill is capable of task-switching, just like the computers which are performing multi-tasking functions. What if ADD Hunters are capable of doing more than one thing at a time—that it's hard-wired into them—and is part of those "alert in the woods" survival skills: walk, listen to sounds, sniff the air, scan between the trees, prepare the weapon, all at the same time?

If Bill and Betty (the Hunters) are capable of easily switching tasks like multi-tasking computers do and we call this attention deficit disorder, then perhaps John (the Farmer) is suffering from a Task-Switching Deficit Disorder (TSDD).

Consider the case of Frederick, who's apparently afflicted with TSDD:

He sat down at his home desk to begin writing a marketing manual for a client. It was just after dinner, and he planned to work for an hour or so. "It was two in the morning when I suddenly realized that I'd been writing for seven hours straight," Frederick said. "My wife and kids had gone to bed, and I hadn't even noticed."

Frederick also claims that he can't work in a quiet place. "I must have a radio or television on when I'm working, otherwise I actually get nervous. I need the stimulation, or I vanish into the job I'm working on and can't climb out for hours."

The problem for Frederick isn't that he can concentrate too much or too easily, but that he can't easily control his concentration. His normal, baseline state of concentration is focused, and he has difficulty turning it off.

Many Hunters describe this same phenomenon—the ability to totally escape into a particular area of focused concentration—but they report it as an *abnormal* or episodic state of consciousness. It's a state some Hunters describe as "being on." (One Hunter adult told me he'd always thought of that state as being "on the jazz," but had never before shared that phrase with anybody else.) There also appear to be subtle differences between the way Hunters and Farmers experience focused consciousness.

Here's how one Hunter described it: "When I'm 'on,' it's not just one thing, it's three! Today was one of those days: from 1:00 p.m. to 6:00 p.m., I was putting together a complex application for a client in Minnesota, writing the documentation for it, creating and running alpha test files on a new printer and writing the alpha report for another client in New Hampshire, and regularly interacting with people via CompuServe. This is a very familiar situation—doing three things at once on different computers. It actually feels physically satisfying, I must say. I remember this feeling way back in '75 working for a big typesetting company. I'd love being there alone at night because I could get all the machines humming at once.

"So perhaps I shift states rather thoroughly. When I get working, time becomes immaterial and I can spin and juggle without difficulty. When I'm 'on,' it is most definitely what you describe as focused, but it's not just one task, it's multi-tasking. All those sounds do blend into a gray shroud, but the bright light illuminates the *mix* of tasks."

(Adult Hunters who take Ritalin report that the drug gives them the ability to "switch on" the focused state with little effort, but that the Ritalin-focused state is not a multi-tasking focused state: attention is directed to one single thing. Many describe this as being the first time in their lives they could control this state of consciousness, or enter a single-point focused state for more than a few minutes at a time—which probably accounts for the common reports of life-transforming experiences as a result of using this drug. The literature of Transcendental Meditation (available from that group nationwide), which teaches how to switch on a focused state without drugs, is similarly filled with studies documenting how people transformed their working and/or personal lives by learning how to activate single-task focused consciousness at will.)

Some Farmers, similarly, are capable of experiencing open consciousness and multi-tasking. For extreme Farmers, though—those suffering from TSDD—this is as difficult as the challenge of remaining in a focused state for an hour is to an ADD Hunter.

Ralph, another TSDD victim and a respected psychotherapist, reports difficulty driving and talking at the same time. When driving and in conversation, he's likely to unthinkingly swerve out of his lane when trying to make an important point, or when mentally struggling with a complex concept. "I'm terrible that way," he reports. "I'm simply constitutionally incapable of doing two things at one time, and my wife won't drive with me because of it."

It's interesting to note that both Frederick and Ralph are married to women whom they describe as "highly distractible." Frederick reports that his wife, who's a surgeon, can't stand to have the radio or television on unless she's directly watching or listening to it; she craves silence when she wants to concentrate or relax. Ralph says the same of his wife; when she's working, she goes into her home office, closes, and sometimes even locks the door so he won't be tempted to distract her.

Ralph and Frederick, on the other hand, both prefer music in the background, or a television on in the room, regardless of what they're doing. Conversely, many Hunters report that the only music they can tolerate (if any) when working is music without words (although this is certainly not a universal comment, and is in no way a diagnostic criterion).

Many ADD/TSDD couples report this incompatibility. While they often support each other's "disorders" by the ADD person bringing excitement and variety to the relationship and the TSDD person supplying patience and stability, their ways of relaxing and working are totally different. Until they realize that one is a Hunter and the other a Farmer—that there are definite differences in the way they use and experience their consciousness—each may simply think the other is being eccentric or difficult. "Why can't he drive while he's talking?" Ralph's wife asks. "Why does my wife get so upset when I want the television on and nobody's watching it?" Frederick asks.

If there's a bell curve to behaviors as postulated earlier, with extreme ADD Hunters on one end, it should be no surprise that severely TSDD Farmers should inhabit the other end. Fortunately for the Farmers, the problems that come out of TSDD are rarely as socially or educationally destructive as those of ADD. Farmers with TSDD may burn-out their working companions with their ability to engage in lengthy meetings on a single subject, or may seem "boring" or "obsessed," but TSDD seems to be a condition better suited to successfully completing school and plugging into the corporate world.

Pediatric neurologist Marcel Kinsbourne, M.D., in his landmark work *Overfocusing: An Apparent Subtype of Attention Deficit-Hyperactivity Disorder*, detailed the characteristics of what this book calls TSDD. In this article, and a previous book published by Little, Brown in 1979 called *Children's Learning and Attention Problem*, Dr. Kinsbourne referred to the condition as "overfocusing." He also gave several examples of the condition and the way it affects the lives of sufferers. Suggesting that ADD may be, in some environments, an adaptive behavior, Dr. Kinsbourne points out that the overfocused state which he has observed in numerous patients is probably the other end of the curve of hereditary behaviors, both of which, *in this society and culture*, are no longer adaptive but, rather, maladaptive.

CULTURAL TRAINING OF OPEN AND FOCUSED AWARENESS

There are apparently two distinctly different positional states into which we can direct normal waking consciousness: *open* and *focused.*

With focused consciousness, a person is totally on

a task, absolutely absorbed in it. The ticking of the clock, the droning of the television, the sounds from the street or the next office all vanish into a gray background, as the bright light of consciousness illuminates only the single task.

Open consciousness, on the other hand, is diffused. The mind wanders from thing to thing, touching one after another lightly, keeping what's interesting, discarding the rest, then wandering to another input. Attention touches the ticking of the clock, which triggers a childhood memory of Uncle Ralph's grandfather clock, which makes you think of those odd ties Uncle Ralph used to wear. That thought's interrupted by the sound of a truck rumbling by on the street outside, which reminds you of the time your father took you for a ride in the truck he'd rented to move household items to a new neighborhood when you were a child.

Everybody has experienced both open and focused awareness. The difference between Farmers and Hunters seems to be the *baseline* state, or the state of consciousness to which the person automatically reverts, when he or she is not trying to maintain one state or the other. Farmers naturally relax into the focused state; Hunters relax into the open state.

An interesting historical anecdote here pertains to the different ways that cultures have trained their members to shift states from open to focused or vice-versa:

The agricultural farmers of Tibet, China, and Japan developed variations on the meditation technique mentioned earlier in the book called Vipassana or *mindfulness*. With this technique, the meditator seeks to empty his or her mind, touching thoughts when they bubble up so that they'll be released and not become a "focus of attention." This technique, practiced for thousands of years in Buddhist monasteries, is a way of training a normally focused person to develop a highly fine-tuned, purely open state of consciousness.

The hunting and warrior cultures of medieval Europe, on the other hand, developed a form of meditation which involved bringing the mind to a single focus, training it to stay with one thought. Passing beads between one's fingers to serve as "reminders" to bring the thought back to the prayer, the meditator would repeat: "Hail Mary, full of grace, the Lord is with Thee..." Similarly, the warrior caste of India developed a meditation technique called Mantra Yoga, which involves repeating a single sound over and over in the mind, for hours at a time, drawing the mind to a single point of focus. (The most famous of these sounds is "Om.")

It's interesting to see how different individuals gravitate to one or the other of these two meditation techniques. Farmers find the Focusing techniques of Mantra Yoga to be easy but, in my experience, they don't stick with them for years at a time. Perhaps this is because they're merely practicing bringing about a state of consciousness which is already pretty routine for them; there's no powerful new insight or experience.

But the sure-and-steady Farmer personality-types seem to predominate at the American, Chinese, and Japanese Buddhist monasteries I've visited. It's almost as if they know the value of training themselves to drop into an open state of consciousness, and enjoy or crave the experience because it's so unique to them.

And, as one might expect, the reverse is true for

people committed to mantra or rosary meditation: they seem more often to be Hunters, who enjoy and/or need the periodic disciplined excursion into the realm of focused consciousness.

Discussing this subject with a senior executive of a major Japanese company in America (he's also native Japanese, who's lived in the United States for about four years), he observed:

"Japan has historically been a farming culture. It was important that everybody show up for planting on the right day at the right time, when the moon and weather were perfect. Each person would have his line of rice to plant, and each sprout had to be placed in the right row, in the right way, at the right time. The survival of our people depended on our being able to perform as a group, with no deviations, and with attention totally concentrated on that one task."

He went on to point out that, in his experience, ADD-type behaviors were very rare in Japan, and told me that there's currently a best-selling book in Japan about how the Japanese culture has evolved as the natural product of an agricultural society. Without extensive research, it's impossible to know if the low reported incidence of ADD in Japan is the result of a lack of awareness of the condition, or of a lack of ADD-genes (except, perhaps, among the descendants of the Samurai?). Or if culture is such a powerful shaping influence that Hunter and Farmer, ADD and TSDD, behaviors are, to a lesser or greater extent, also the result of the societal conditioning.

Some researchers believe that the recent explosion in ADD diagnoses is a result of an increased sensitivity to the condition coinciding with a deterioration in our public schools' ability to deal with ADD children (largely because underfunding has increased class sizes). Others argue that technology drives culture, and that our *society* is now more likely to produce ADD-type people because of technological changes in the past forty years.

Marie Winn, in her book *The Plug-In Drug*, argues that an inability to concentrate is the natural result of the proliferation of television. She points out that fifty years ago children spent much of their lifetimes practicing the focused process of reading for entertainment. Today, they frequently spend hours every day watching television, which rarely maintains an image or a concept for more than a few moments, which, she claims, "trains" a short attention span. Home video games may have a similar effect.

PHYSICAL VERSUS MENTAL EVOLUTIONARY ADAPTIVE CHANGES

There is considerable evidence that Tay-Sachs, sickle-cell anemia, and even the dreaded cystic fibrosis are genetic conditions which developed as survival mechanisms in response to specific times and conditions. Hereditary size aids survival in a primitive society, where the biggest warrior lives to pass on his genetic code, or where the small man consumes fewer calories during a famine, or can hide more easily in the jungle or forest. While child-onset diabetes is usually caused by a destructive infection of cells in the pancreas, there's some evidence that adult-onset diabetes is an inherited condition and (perhaps like the genetic predisposition to obesity) may play some part in surviving episodic famines.

Much has been written over the years about *physical* dysfunctions representing the natural evolution of

survival mechanisms. But what about *mental* dysfunctions? There's a very close link between mind and
body. If the same evolutionary variation takes place in
the brain, then perhaps some abnormal mental states
had a valid historical use. Just as the Hunter state
equips a person for a particular kind of survival, perhaps other mental states let the brain "tune in" to
perceptions that aren't accessible to most of us.

It seems strange that the breakdown of normal
consciousness could be accompanied by accurate insights, but it happens. I personally knew a woman who
(as she entered schizophrenia) had some startling insights. And I sat with some old men from a primitive
culture as they recited facts they had no apparent way
of knowing—while they engaged in a bizarre ritual.
Here are those stories.

DEBBY THE VISIONARY ARTIST

Debby was a wonderful woman and a good friend. I'll
never forget the evening she came to my apartment,
while we were both in college, to tell me that the moon
was revealing the future of the world to her. We walked
outside and sat on the cool grass all night discussing
the fate of mankind, the nature of creativity, and the
voices she was hearing within her head whenever she
performed a secret and magical series of hand motions.
The moon was warning us, she said, that man was
poisoning the earth. All the killing in Vietnam (this was
in 1968) was creating a pain in the collective human
psyche which would echo through generations. A hole
would be burned in the sky by our toxic chemicals,
one day making the planet unlivable. The great world
power that we needed to worry about was not the
Soviet Union, but Germany, where the Nazis would rise

again before the end of the twentieth century. And Bill, our friend who played the guitar so beautifully, would be dead one day soon (he died a year later).

Assuming that Debby had taken some of the then-omnipresent LSD, I baby-sat my friend through her trip, listening to her often-profound insights into the human condition, the future of the world, the history of ancient man, and intelligence among the stars. Frequently, she lapsed into long, rambling episodes, whose logic was so buried in meaning only accessible to her mind, layer within layer, that I was totally lost. But I nodded, or agreed, or held her hand when her insights struck her with an occasional terror.

Debby was a brilliant artist and writer. That night she composed some short poetry and created some sketches (now, alas, forever lost) which, to my young mind, rivaled T.S. Eliot and Salvador Dali. Her work was brilliant—rich in subtle meaning, filled with details that became profound when Debby explained them.

The next day, Debby did not "come down." Sometime during the night before, she'd called her mother to share one particularly powerful "insight," and her mother had called a psychiatrist. Within a day, Debby was in a psychiatric hospital, diagnosed as schizophrenic. (It turned out she had never taken the LSD that I'd assumed was driving her behavior.) Medicated to a thick docility, she'd lost both the joy and the terror of her voices and insights, and begged me to finish one of her poems, a job I worked on for a week with little success. It was *her* glimpse into another world that the poem sought to recreate, which I could only blandly describe.

It took about five years of Thorazine and lithium and various other drugs for Debby to "come back to

normal." The diagnosis of schizophrenia was confirmed several times and, it was found, the disease
apparently ran in her family. With medication, she now
has a child and teaches art in an elementary school,
and no longer hears the voice of the moon.

THE UGANDAN "TOUCHED BY THE GODS"

In 1980, James Mbutu (an Episcopal priest and mem-
ber of the interim cabinet of the Ugandan government)
and I traveled in an old taxi (missing a windshield and
right-hand door, the trunk and back seat filled with
cans of gasoline and boxes of wheat), through central
Uganda, past the mouth of the Nile River at Lake
Victoria, and up to the famine-ravaged Karamoja region. When Idi Amin and his 20,000 soldiers fled the
region a few months earlier (they were driven from the
country by the then-occupying Tanzanians), they'd
passed this way, robbing, raping, and killing. Particularly hard-hit were the simple nomadic people of the
extreme north, the Karamajong, who lived by drinking
blood and milk from the cows they herded in the
desert-like scrub land, a thousand-mile strip separating
the jungle of Uganda to the south from the desert and
mountains of Ethiopia and Sudan to the north.

At one refugee camp just north of Jinja, James and
I visited a gathering of the elders, a group of old men
who had somehow escaped the slaughter of Amin's
troops (the pattern had been kill the men, rape the
women, steal the food). The sun was setting and a
bitter smoke cut into my nose from the many tiny
campfires; the air was about 50 degrees, and women
and children everywhere were huddled under tarps or
blankets to escape the cold. The obvious tuberculosis
and cholera victims were segregated in the corners of

the camp under the watchful eye of an Irish woman from the Red Cross. (Her name was Ann, and she was killed by a sniper's bullet a month later. I've never met a braver or more compassionate person.) And, in the morning, an old Ethiopian priest led us in the task of digging mass graves and burying the bodies of those who had died of disease or starvation during the night.

But that first night I witnessed an extraordinary event. I was one of only seventeen whites in the entire nation (Amin had run all "foreigners" out two years earlier in a "purge"), and the old men of the tribe asked James to invite me to their evening ceremony. About a dozen ancient, withered, toothless men sat in a circle around a large gourd filled with a milky, fermented liquid. One man, bizarre images painted onto his face with charcoal and plant dye, walked from person to person with a ten-foot bamboo straw, giving us drinks from the gourd, which James said was a fermented mixture made by chewing a local root, then spitting the chewed mixture into the pot, where it was left in the sun to brew into a potent alcoholic mixture. Other herbs from the jungle were added in, and, James said, "the effect can be rather powerful."

A few minutes later, the medicine man walked around the circle and waved a burning bundle of herbs in each of our faces. He then sat and rambled for an hour or two in Swahili and broken English about Idi Amin, looking into the "spirit world" to tell us where Amin was and what he was doing. Amin would live like a king in Saudi Arabia, the man said, and a plague would befall Uganda. He held conversations with invisible spirits, occasionally jumping up and screaming, dancing around the circle.

Remembering my friend Debby, I turned to James,

who held a masters degree in psychology as part of his divinity studies. "Schizophrenic?" I asked.

James shrugged. "He throws bones. Sees the future. Heals people. Here, they would say he has been touched by the gods."

In medieval Europe, I thought, they would have said he was touched by a demon and burned him at the stake. The Native Americans of the Southwest might have elevated him to greatness as a medicine man. If he could write, in another culture he might be called a Nostradamus; if he could paint, a Van Gogh. Here, then, is another trait that is occasionally adaptive and furthers a culture, but more often is maladaptive and destroys the individual.

Several psychiatrists have mentioned the popular notion that ADD is a dopamine deficiency in the frontal lobes of the brain. It's popular, particularly in books which are trying to destigmatize the condition for children, to use diabetes and insulin therapy as an analogy.

This analogy, of course, presupposes some sort of desirable norm. Had Edison, Franklin, Nostradamus, Handel, Dali, Ford, Mozart, Hemingway, or Van Gogh been medicated back to "normal," the world might well be a very different and far less interesting place. On the other hand, had such normalizing medication been available during childhood to the huge percentage of ADD adults in our prisons, much human suffering might been eliminated, lives saved, and our society might well be a safer and more comfortable place to live.

THE "DRUG ABUSE/ALCOHOLISM/ADD GENE"

The United States of America, a country that some cultural anthropologists could argue was most recently

conquered by ADD-gene-carrying northern Europeans, recently surpassed South Africa as having the
highest per-capita prison population in the world. A
significant majority of these crimes are drug-related,
which brings us back to the original question posed:
Are Hunters mental diabetics? Are ADD people actually genetically deficient in dopamine and/or other
essential brain chemicals, or the receptors to them?
And, if so, does this mean that the simple act of admin-
istering widespread medication to Hunters will, ultimately, cure many of our social ills? Might it also
provide a cure for that significant subpopulation of
alcoholics and drug addicts who resist any form of
group or individual therapy for their addiction?

David E. Comings, M.D., et al., found a specific
gene which appears to have a relationship to alcoholism, drug abuse, Tourette's Syndrome, and ADD. This
gene, the A1 variant of the D2 dopamine receptor gene,
appears more than twice as often in people with ADD
as it does in "normal" individuals, and controls the
ability of certain cells in the brain, called receptor sites,
to be sensitive to dopamine (producing the effect of a
deficiency of dopamine). Among Tourette's Syndrome
sufferers, the ratio of the presence of this gene is almost
four-to-one compared to the general population. Interestingly, among alcoholics and severe drug abusers,
prevalence of this gene variant is over eight-to-one.

This returns us to the difficult notion of how to
view, treat, and, perhaps most important, how to present to children, the concept of ADD. Many books on
the subject, particularly those written for children,
treat it as a purely medical condition. They discuss
kids' questions like "How did I catch ADD?" and "Can
other people catch ADD from me?" which serve to

reinforce in the child's mind the notion that she or he is somehow diseased or defective. Since most of this literature is written by medical professionals, it shouldn't be surprising that any condition or deviation from the norm would be viewed in the medical-model context as a disease. Many parents, and some therapists, however, are uncomfortable telling a child that she or he has a mental disease, and must, therefore, take drugs, perhaps for the rest of his or her life.

On the other hand, drug intervention for ADD Hunters, like that for schizophrenics (who, in another culture, may have been saints or mystics), can sometimes be life-saving. Particularly for those Hunters who have spent much of their life in fruitless, dangerous, and often illegal attempts at self-medication, appropriate therapeutic, pharmacological intervention may be a huge relief.

Some books on the subject have now taken the diabetes/insulin approach to describing ADD, rather than the mental-illness/take-a-drug model. This is certainly more constructive for a child trying to understand the nature of his difference from his peers, but it still raises troubling societal questions—particularly when one remembers the graphed incidence of the A1 variant dopamine receptor gene, and its correlative frequency of drug abuse. If the desire for drugs is genetic, is it ultimately impossible to stop drug abuse? And while Van Gogh's mental and emotional agony, leading him to cut off an ear and ultimately commit suicide, may have been eliminated by proper medication, would we all really be the better for his having been "normalized?"

Answering questions about the appropriateness of drug decriminalization, or getting into the political/religious arena of determinism versus free choice when discussing the actions of addicts, compulsives, or offenders, is beyond the scope of this book. But it is indeed thought-provoking to take a detailed look at the statistics which suggest a genetic basis to ADD, its apparent statistical correlation to a craving for drugs or alcohol, and the significant numbers of people with ADD who are either in prison or, alternately, are among the most famous of our society's creative, political, or business leaders.

In the context of a discussion of ADD, however, the important point of this chapter is the notion of baseline states of consciousness.

If one were to imagine a 12-inch ruler balanced on a finger at the 6-inch point as representing the spectrum of consciousness, then extremely focused consciousness may appear at the 2-inch area. Extremely open consciousness is represented by the 10-inch area. At 6 inches is the center point, into which the "average" person falls when relaxing. A Hunter may relax into the 7- or 8-inch area as a norm, whereas a Farmer may relax into the 5- or 4-inch area. And, some have speculated, an autistic person may be at the 1-inch area, or a schizophrenic may be stuck at 12 inches.

While this is extremely simplistic and doesn't take into account the variety of overlapping levels of genetic predispositions, neurotransmitter levels, etc. (particularly when discussing autism and schizophrenia), it's still a useful model for viewing ADD and task-switching deficit disorder.

This paradigm also gives us a model to appreciate and even celebrate the diversity of the human family, rather than immediately labeling the differences between people in a socially pejorative fashion. Learning to focus, or learning to open up, takes on a new meaning when viewed in this context. It suggests that non-drug methods, such as meditation or the restriction of access to television for children, can be therapeutic without side effects, cost, or particular difficulty. It also shows us how those who choose to use drugs to make themselves more Farmer-like are not necessarily "mentally ill."

By reframing the entire discussion of ADD and ADHD from one of mental illness to one of normal, explainable human differences, we can provide relief and offer solutions.

Relief is due those people who know they have ADD but who are embarrassed by the current social stigma of having a "deficit" or a "disorder." They are not ill, nor are they deficient: they're Hunters, and most of the problems they encounter in modern society come from their Hunter's instincts clashing with our culture's Farmer's norms. Heirs to "the Edison Trait," as a group they retain vast potential which, in many cases, is unexploited by our society.

The solution—indeed, the salvation for children who are struggling through school or adults who cringe at the "daily grind"—is to re-set the stage.

Hunter children in our schools need Hunter-based classrooms. Smaller classes, more experience-based learning and visual aids, and fewer distractions will nurture hidden talents and, often, brilliance in children who are now failing or whose potential is stunted by the anti-Hunter systems in our schools.

For adults, the solution is to find a workplace that provides the stimulation and change they need. ADD adults need to recognize the things that they may never do particularly well, shifting their efforts, instead, to those things at which they can easily excel.

The first step is for our schools, our workplaces, and our health care professionals to view this continuum of behavioral differences from a Hunter/Farmer, "Edison Trait" perspective. Reformulating our views and systems on this basis will make millions of lives more productive, and our society as a whole will benefit from the liberation of thousands of potential Tom Edisons and Ben Franklins.

Older and Younger Cultures: Further Thoughts on Cultural Anthropology and Our Future

In all of my books on ADD I have pointed out that survival skills persisting from prehistoric times, when our ancestors were hunter-gatherers and scavangers, are now problems in many modern schools or workplaces. I have elaborated on this perception, which for some people depicts a history where noble Hunters have been systematically destroyed by the encroachment of ignoble Farmers.*

While it is true that there are now very few hunting societies left on the Earth, the real paradigm is deeper than just Hunters vs. Farmers.

That model does a fine job of explaining why some kids excel or fail in school, or why high-stimulation-seeking people are drawn to jobs like being an emergency

*Much of this material first appeared in my book *The Prophets Way.*

medical technician while low-stimulation-seeking people are drawn to jobs like accounting, but it misses a
larger and more important point. Prophets from
Jeremiah to Jesus to Nostradamus to Edgar Cayce have
pointed out to us that "modern" (post-agricultural revolution, since 10,000 BCE) humankind is destroying
the world in which we live.

A common explanation put forth for this is that
there is a basic flaw in human nature. This concept of
Original Sin is said to be depicted in the biblical story
of Eve and the apple in Eden, where this defect suppos-
edly orignated.

One problem with this concept is that there have
been human societies around for hundreds of thousands of years—people not too different from you and
me—who have not acted destructively. Instead, they
have lived in harmony with nature.

I first encountered this understanding more than
thirty years ago, reading Margaret Mead's book *Coming
of Age in Samoa.* But there are good counter-arguments
to her view of the noble primitive, and it seemed to me
then that her Samoan "primitive" people were lacking
basic and important things like advanced medical care
and communications—things which would have improved their lives.

My assumption then was that our culture, what we
call Western Civilization, was inherently better and more
valuable than the "primitive" cultures which preceded it.

Recently I became aware of cultures exemplified by
the ancient Kogi tribe who live far up in the Andes
mountains. The Kogi people call themselves Elder
Brothers and they have existed in harmony with the
world for thousands of years. They tread lightly upon
this Earth and even their architecture has not damaged

the local ecosystems. In terms of the Hunter/Farmer metaphor, the Elder Brother people exhibit characteristics of Farmers. But I had been mentally blaming Farmers for much of the mess of modern civilization.

If some Farming cultures have lived peacefully and acted as caretakers of the earth, they apparently possess knowledge or wisdom which we moderns lack. But how could primitive people who survive on simple cereal crops have anything to teach civilized men and women? We have, after all, conquered the Earth. We have conquered disease, hunger, space, and even the atom.

If some ancient civilizations have lived in accord with the world as Farmers, without creating a "civilization" that (like other Farmer societies of Europe, Africa, and Asia) would ultimately lead to the death of the world, what was different about them?

How could it be that some Farmer peoples would leave behind a planet relatively unscathed, whereas others would wreak such incredible damage that it would put all life on Earth at risk?

I had similarly paradoxical questions about Hunters. Many primitive Hunting people (using my metaphor) left only gentle footprints on the planet. Elaborate cave paintings from 30,000 years ago in France, and 20,000 years ago in Australia are the remnants they have left us: not piles of nuclear waste which will be lethal for over a million years into the future.

But other Hunting people were exploitative. They burned forests to drive out animals, or, more commonly, turned their hunting efforts against their neighbors and became hunters of humans. The Mongols and Tartars, originally nomadic hunting tribes, rose to conquer most of Europe and ruled it with a brutal iron fist for centuries, every bit as cruelly as had the Roman empire which had evolved from an agricultural society.

ADD may to a large extent be something as simple as Hunter and Farmer material remnant in our genetic code. But more can be learned and finer distinctions can be made by considering the idea that cultures may be characterized as "Old" and "Young." The Old Cultures, be they agricultural or hunting/gathering, live with an intrinsic connection to the Earth. For them, the planet on which we live is itself a living organism. It has its own life, its own destiny, and, in a way that the Younger Cultures could never understand, its own consciousness. Things that run counter to the Earth's nature will (naturally) not work in the long run—although the damage may be too slow to be noticeable on the Younger Culture time scale. To tell which culture is which, we need only look at what is happening on the planet. What I have seen in my own travels is very disturbing.

The Younger Cultures view themselves as separate from the Earth, with "dominion" over it. They see the resources of Earth as things to be used and then discarded. Nature is often the enemy, not the mother, father, or brother/sister of these Younger peoples. Their disregard for it is so visceral, so intrinsic to their world-view, that many live their entire lives without ever once questioning their own cultural assumptions about man's place in the universe.

The Older peoples are so clear in their understanding of humankind's place on Earth that they often pray for the soul of an animal as they kill it for food. They may daily thank G-d for the life given them, and the life around them, all of which is viewed with reverence.

The Younger peoples, on the other hand, are so

egocentric that they have tenaciously fought—killed and tortured—to preserve their belief that our planet is at the center of all creation. They make it an article of faith to seek out and convert Older Cultures to their view of the world ... or obliterate them entirely, as was done to indigenous tribes across much of North and South America, Africa, Australia, and Europe.

Currently, Older Cultures the world over are warning Younger Cultures of the danger and stupidity of their ways. We have only to listen.

This may seem far afield of a discussion of ADD and its causes, but no one can travel in the world today with open eyes and fail to see an ongoing escalation of social and ecological destruction. Drastic solutions are called for. We need to change our way of living, or perish. Historically, necessary transformational changes in our culture have been brought about by misfits, malcontents, and dropouts—people like Thomas Edison and Benjamin Franklin. Perhaps some of our young Hunters, who we view as having difficulty in school and with adjustment to our society, will be the ones to show us new ways into a new future.

A final thought from two decades ago

—

"There are approximately five million children who are considered to be hyperactive children in this country. There has been a great deal of concern and interest as to the best way and means of treating these young children.

"It has been brought to the attention of the subcommittees in recent times about certain drugs that were being required to be administered to children in order for the children to go to school....

"I understand that schoolteachers are the ones who are making the decision about the need of the children to take that particular drug (methylphenidate or Ritalin). This drug is given in order for the child to be able to continue in the classroom. That is the way I read that.

"It is not a doctor who is doing the deciding (although doctors are doing the prescribing). Irrespective of what perhaps you and I believe about the overutilization of those drugs among children, it is not even a doctor, but it is a school official who requires the parent to administer that drug to the child in order to participate in the classroom.

"The question about the teachers themselves making those decisions is very interesting. I think any of us who see children, who have children or who have a lot of nieces and nephews, know they are fidgety, anxious, and maybe bored in some of their classrooms. Now we have a situation— at least in this reported area— where a schoolteacher who has some children who might not be as interested, who may be a little bored with the classroom, can require the children to take a drug in order to stay in the classroom.

"I'm not sure that that is a very hopeful or helpful sign."

— Senator Edward M. Kennedy, Chairman, in his opening remarks and discussion with Dr. Ben Feingold before the Subcommittee on Health, Committee on Labor and Public Welfare, hearings on "Examination into the Causes of Hyperactive Children..." 1975

A final thought from Dave deBronkart:

One hears of life passing before the eyes as death approaches, but I suspect that is not quite what is happening. Rather, we may always have all those moments of our lives available to us, but we block most of them out.

With this in mind, for decades I've had an urge to open up, to be present in all times of my life at once.

One function of consciousness may be to take the totality of all-at-once time and separate it into a string of apparently unconnected moments, so that each moment can be dealt with separately. This can be useful, but it comes at a price: to deal with a single moment, you give up being present in *all* moments.

There may be good reason for "Hunters" to have a time-sense that is different from what we think of as the norm. The goal of hunting is to bring pertinent things together at once. What matters is that the hunter and the weapon and the prey are converging, so you need the ability to synchronize all the cues. "Farmers," in contrast, need the ability to see what leads to what, in a much more distant future.

To a Hunter with an "all at once" mind, it may seem pretty silly to try to get food by putting seeds in the dirt and walking away. But for a Farmer who experiences time in a "this leads to that" sequence, it is exactly the right thing to do.

Perhaps the hunter/farmer difference is, among other things, a difference in how we experience time. The farmer's time emphasizes patience and "first things first." Many Hunters see things as "Now" (part of this time) or "Not now." And if you expand Now enough, you experience the whole of your life ... all at once.

About the Author

—

by Dave deBronkart

In the opening paragraph of Chapter Thirteen, the author wrote: Hunters sometimes have difficulty answering the question *What do you do for a living?* It's not that there isn't an answer: there are too many answers.

That statement easily applies to his own life, and shows that ADD need not keep a person from success.

Thomas Hartmann has worked with hundreds of ADD and hyperactive children and adults over the past twenty years. In 1978, he and his wife Louise opened the New England Salem Children's Village (NESCV), a residential treatment facility for children on one hundred and thirty-two wooded acres on Stinson Lake in New Hampshire. The Children's Village is based on the family model of the international Salem program located in Germany.

As executive director of NESCV for five years, Hartmann worked with numerous psychologists and psychiatrists, social workers and courts, and hundreds of children and parents. He taught parenting classes, helped train child-care workers, was co-founder of the New Hampshire Group Home Association, and worked closely with that state's governor to develop programs for children in crisis.

NESCV specializes in providing previously institutionalized children with a family model, non-institutional setting, and works, usually, without drugs with children who have nearly all been in some form of drug therapy. It was the subject of three major reports on National Public Radio's *All Things Considered* afternoon news program, as well as feature articles in *Parenting, Prevention, East-West, Country Journal*, and over a dozen other national publications and newspapers.

175

Hartmann also worked with the international Salem program based in Europe to set up famine relief and other, similar programs in Africa, Europe, South America, and Asia, and lived with his family for a year in Germany at the international Salem headquarters. In Uganda, in 1980 (just months after Idi Amin was run out of the country), he entered a war zone and negotiated with the provisional government for land to build a hospital and refugee center, which is still operating and seeing an average of over five hundred patients a day. He has helped set up similar programs in several other countries, most recently traveling to Bogotá, Colombia.

From 1972 to 1978, and 1987 to 1991, he taught concentration and meditation techniques through a series of weekly classes, and spoke on these subjects at numerous conferences in the United States and Europe.

As a journalist, Hartmann spent seven years as a radio and television news reporter during and immediately after his college years, and has been published over two hundred times in more than fifty different national and international publications, ranging from the German version of *International Business Week* and *The Christian Science Monitor*, to *Popular Computing*, for which he wrote a monthly column for two years. At one time he was Contributing Editor to, and a columnist for, seven different national magazines, and he is the winner of the prestigious Jessie H. Neal award for excellence in reporting. His monograph about dietary intervention in the hyperactive syndrome was published in 1981 in *The Journal of Orthomolecular Psychiatry*, and one of his short stories won a national award.

Additionally, Hartmann has successfully started seven businesses, one of which made the front page of *The Wall Street Journal*. Enterprises he has started (and, with two exceptions, later sold) include an advertising agency, a newsletter/magazine publishing company, an herbal tea manufacturing company, an international travel wholesaler and travel agency, a training company presenting seminars nationwide, an electronics design and repair company, and a company which sells computer peripherals. He has written nine novels, is both a licensed pilot and a licensed private detective (neither of which he practices), and a former skydiver.

The founder of the Michigan Healing Arts Center, and a student of "alternative" medicine, he received a C.H. (Chartered Herbalist) degree from Dominion Herbal College, an M.H. (Master of Herbology) degree from Emerson College, and a Ph.D. in Homeopathic Medicine from Brantridge in England (his Ph.D. thesis was published in a national-circulation magazine in the United States, and these degrees qualify him to practice homeopathic and herbal medicine in England, Canada, India, and several other countries). He also completed a residential post-graduate course in acupuncture at the Beijing International Acupuncture Institute, the world's largest accredited acupuncture teaching hospital, in Beijing, China, in 1986.

A student of technology, he held a radio and TV station broadcast engineering license from the federal government, is a former amateur radio operator, a Certified Electronics Technician, and a former engineer/technician for RCA.

He currently holds contracts with the CompuServe Information Service to supervise and operate the Desktop Publishing and DTP Vendor Forums, Office Automation Forum, ADD Forum, International Trade Forum, and half a dozen others. In this capacity, he daily helps serve the needs of CompuServe's millions of members, and can easily be reached online at 76702,765 or www.mythical.net. His books about ADD, business and spirituality are available in bookstores nationwide.

In the marketing and advertising field (his specialty), he is the former partner in an advertising agency, the current president of three active companies including a news-letter publishing company, a consultant to hundreds of companies, and has taught seminars on advertising and marketing to over ten thousand companies and individuals in the past fifteen years. His clients include over four hundred and seventy of the Fortune 500 firms, and he has been a keynote speaker to groups ranging from a Hong Kong banker's meeting, to a forum on international travel sponsored by KLM Airlines and American Express in Amsterdam, to the California Teachers Association's annual conference. He has spoken to over 100,000 people on four continents.

An inveterate traveler and sometimes a risk-taker, Hartmann has often found himself in the world's hot spots on behalf of the Salem organization or as a writer, a situation which causes his friends to sometimes wonder aloud if he works for the CIA (he does not). He was, for example, in The Philippines when Ferdinand Marcos fled the country; in Egypt the week Anwar Sadat was shot; in Uganda during the war of liberation by Tanzania; in Hungary when the first East German refugees arrived; in Germany when the wall came down; in Peru when the Shining Path first bombed the presidential palace; in Beijing during the first student demonstrations; in Thailand when they were briefly invaded by Laos, then again when the military coup of 1991 occurred, then again when the military were thrown out in 1992; in Barbados during the recent anti-government strikes and shutdowns; in Bogotá and Medellin, Colombia, during the spate of killings of presidential candidates; in Israel, in the West Bank town of Nablus, the week the Intifada started there; on the Czech border the week Chernobyl melted down; in Kenya during the first big wave of crackdowns on dissidents; and in Venezuela during the 1991 coup attempt.

Hartmann is a certified and licensed NLP Practitioner and NLP Trainer.

Born in 1951, he is the father of three children aged sixteen to twenty-three, and has been married to the same (very patient) non-ADD wife for twenty-five years.

Bibliography

American Psychiatric Association. "Tic Disorders." *Treatments of Psychiatric Disorders*, vol. 1. Washington, DC: American Psychiatric Association, 1989.

American Psychiatric Association. *Diagnostic and Statistical Manual of Mental Disorders*. 3rd ed. Washington, D.C.: American Psychiatric Association, 1987.

Anderson, J. C., et al. "DSM-III Disorders in Preadolescent Children. Prevalence in a Large Sample from the General Population." *Archives of General Psychiatry*, 44 (1987), 69-76.

Barkley, R. A., et al. "Development of a Multimethod Clinical Protocol for Assessing Stimulant Drug Response in Children with Attention Deficit Disorder." *Journal of Clinical Child Psychology*, 17 (1988), 14-24.

_____. *Hyperactive Children: A Handbook for Diagnosis and Treatment.* New York: Guilford, 1981.

_____. "The Social Behavior of Hyperactive Children: Developmental Changes, Drug Effects, and Situational Variation." *Childhood Disorders: Behavioral-developmental Approaches*. Edited by R.J. McMahon and R.D. Peters. New York: Brunner/Mazel, 1985.

Bowen, Catherine Drinker. *The Most Dangerous Man in America: Scenes from the Life of Benjamin Franklin*. Boston: Little, Brown & Company, 1974.

Brown, Ronald T., et al. "Effects of Methylphenidate on Cardiovascular Responses in Attention Deficit Hyperactivity Disordered Adolescents." *Journal of Adolescent Health Care*, 10 (1989), 179-183.

Buckley, W. F., Jr. *Overdrive: A Personal Documentary*. New York: Doubleday & Company, 1983.

Burdett, Osbert. *The Two Carlyles*. 1930 repr. 1980.

Campbell, Ian. *Thomas Carlyle*. 1975.

Clubbe, John, ed. *Froude's Life of Carlyle*, 1979.

Comings, D. E., et al. "The Dopamine D2 Receptor Locus as a Modifying Gene in Enuropsychiatric Disorders." *Journal of the American Medical Association*, 266 (1991), 1793-1800.

_____, and Comings, B. G. "Tourette's Syndrome and Attention Deficit Disorder with Hyperactivity: Are They Genetically Related?" *Journal of the American Academy of Child Psychiatry*, 23 (1984), 138-146.

Doyle, Sir Arthur Conan. "The Sign of the Four." *Lippincott's Monthly Magazine*, London, 1890.

Einstein, Albert. *Out of My Later Years*. New York: Bonanza, 1956, 1990.

Evans, R. W., Clay, T. H., and Gualtieri, C. T. "Carbamazepine in Pediatric Psychiatry." *Journal of the American Academy of Child Psychiatry*, 26 (1987), 2-8.

Farwell, Byron. *Burton: A Biography of Sir Richard Francis Burton*. London: Penguin, 1990.

Feingold, Benjamin. *Why Your Child is Hyperactive*. New York: Random House, 1975.

Garber, *et al*. *If Your Child is Hyperactive, Inattentive, Impulsive, Distractible* ... New York: Villard Books, 1990.

Gittelman-Klein, R. "Pharmacotherapy of Childhood Hyperactivity: An Update." *Psychopharmacology: The Third Generation of Progress*. Edited by H. Y. Meltzer. New York: Raven, 1987.

Goyette, C. H., Conners, C. K., and Ulrich, R.F. "Normative Data on Revised Conners Parent and Teacher Rating Scales." *Journal of Abnormal Child Psychology*, 6 (1978), 221-36.

Greenhill, Laurence, *et al*. "Prolactin: Growth Hormone and Growth Responses in Boys with Attention Deficit Disorder and Hyperactivity Treated with Methylphenidate." *Journal of the American Academy of Child Psychiatry*, 23 (1984), 58-67.

Hayes, Peter L. *Ernest Hemingway*. New York: Continuum, 1990.

Henker, B., and Whalen, C.K. "The Changing Faces of Hyperactivity: Retrospect and Prospect." *Hyperactive Children: The Social Ecology of Identification and Treatment*. Edited by B. A. Henker and C. K. Whalen. New York: Academic, 1980.

Josephson, Matthew. *Edison: A Biography*. New York: John Wiley & Sons, 1959, 1992.

Kelly, Kevin L., *et al*. "Attention Deficit Disorder and Methylphenidate: A Multistep Analysis of Dose-Response Effects on Children's Cardiovascular Functioning." *International Clinical Psychopharmacology*, 3 (1988), 167-181.

Kinsbourne, M., and Caplan, P. J. *Children's Learning and Attention Problems*. Boston, MA: Little, Brown and Company, 1979.

_____. "Overfocusing: Attending to a Different Drummer." *Chadder*, 1992.

_____. "Overfocusing: An Apparent Subtype of Attention Deficit-hyperactivity Disorder." *Pediatric Neurology: Behavior and Cognition of the Child with Brain Dysfunction.* Edited by N. Amir, I. Rapin, and D. Branski. Basel: Karger, 1991.

Klein, Rachel G., *et al.* "Methylphenidate and Growth in Hyperactive Children. A Controlled Withdrawal Study." *Archives of General Psychiatry*, 45 (1988), 1127-30.

Kuczenski, R., *et al.* "Effects of Amphetamine, Methylphenidate and Apomorphine on Regional Brain Serotonin and 5-Hydroxyindole Acetic Acid." *Psychopharmacology*, 93 (1987), 329-335.

Lorayne, H., and Lucas, J. *The Memory Book*, New York: Ballantine, 1986.

McGuinness, Diane. "Attention Deficit Disorder, the Emperor's Clothes, Animal Pharm, and Other Fiction." *The Limits of Biological Treatment for Psychological Distress.* Edited by S. Fisher and R. Greenberg. New York: Erlbaum, 1989.

_____. *When Children Don't Learn.* New York: Basic Books, 1985.

Mendelsohn, Robert S., M.D. *How to Raise a Healthy Child ... in Spite of Your Doctor.* Chicago: Contemporary Books, 1984.

"Methylphenidate Effects on Ultimate Height." *Archives of General Psychiatry*, 45 (1988), 1131-34.

Moss, Robert A., and Dunlap, Helen H. *Why Johnny Can't Concentrate.* New York: Bantam Books, 1990.

Murray, John B. "Psychophysiological Effects of Methylphenidate (Ritalin)." *Psychological Reports*, 61 (1987), 315-336.

Peters, T., and Waterman, R. *In Search of Excellence.* New York: Harper & Row 1982.

Rapaport, J. L., *et al.* "Dextroamphetamine: Its Cognitive and Behavioral Effects in Normal and Hyperactive Boys and Normal Men." *Archives of General Psychiatry*, 37 (1980), 933-43.

Rapport, M. D., *et al.* "Attention Deficit Disorder and Methylphenidate: A Multilevel Analysis of Dose-response Effects on Children's Impulsivity Across Settings." *Journal of the American Academy of Child Psychiatry*, 27 (1988), 60-69.

Safer, Daniel J., *et al.* "A Survey of Medication Treatment for Hyperactive/Inattentive Students." *Journal of the American Medical Association*, 260 (1988), 2256-2258.

Satterfield, J. H., Satterfield, B. T., and Schell, A. M. "Therapeutic

Interventions to Prevent Delinquency in Hyperactive Boys." *Journal of the American Academy of Child Psychiatry*, 26 (1987), 56-64.

_____, *et al.* "Growth of Hyperactive Children Treated with Methylphenidate." *Archives of General Psychiatry*, 36 (1979), 212-217.

Scarnati, Richard. "An Outline of Hazardous Side Effects of Ritalin (Methylphenidate)." *The International Journal of Addictions*, 21 (1986).

Shaffer, D., *et al.* "Neurological Soft Signs: Their Relationship to Psychiatric Disorder and Intelligence in Childhood and Adolescence." *Archives of General Psychiatry*, 42 (1985), 342-51.

Sharma, Rajiv P., *et al.* "Pharmacological Effects of Methylphenidate on Plasma Homovanillic Acid and Growth Hormone." *Psychiatry Research*, 32 (1990), 9-17.

Sokol, Mae S., *et al.* "Attention Deficit Disorder with Hyperactivity and the Dopamine Hypothesis: Case Presentations with Theoretical Background." *American Academy of Child and Adolescent Psychiatry*, (1987).

Sternberg, Robert J., and Lubart, Todd L. "Creating Creative Minds." *Phi Delta Kappa*, April, 1991, pp. 608-614.

Stewart, A. "Severe Perinatal Hazards." *Developmental Neuropsychiatry*. Edited by M. Rutter. New York: Guilford, 1983.

Strauss, C. C., *et al.* "Overanxious Disorder: An Examination of Developmental Differences." *Journal of Abnormal Child Psychology*, 16 (1988), 433-43.

Swanson, J. M., and Kinsboume, M. "The Cognitive Effects of Stimulant Drugs on Hyperactive Children." *Attention and Cognitive Development*. Edited by G. A. Hale and M. Lewis. New York: Plenum, 1979.

Taylor, E., *et al.* "Which Boys Respond to Stimulant Medication? A Controlled Trial of Methylphenidate in Boys with Disruptive Behaviour." *Psychology Med*, 17 (1987), 121-43.

Ullmann, R. K., and Sleator, E. K. "Responders, Nonresponders, and Placebo Responders Among Children with Attention Deficit Disorder." *Clinical Pediatrics*, 25 (1986), 594-99.

US Congress. Senate. *Examination Into the Causes of Hyperactive Children and the Methods Used for Treating These Young Children. Joint Hearing* before a Subcommittee on Health of the Committee on Labor and Public Welfare and the Subcommittee on Administrative Practice and Procedure of the Committee on the Judiciary of the United States Senate, 94th Cong, 1st sess., September 11, 1975. US Government Printing Office.

Weiss, G., and Hechtman, L. T. *Hyperactive Children Grown Up: Empirical Findings and Theoretical Considerations.* New York: Guilford, 1986.

Weizman, Ronit, *et al.* "Effects of Acute and Chronic Methylphenidate Administration of B-Endorphin, Growth Hormone Prolactin and Cortisol in Children with Attention Deficit Disorder and Hyperactivity." *Life Sciences,* 40 (1987), 2247-2252.

Wender, P. H. *Minimal Brain Dysfunction in Children.* New York: Wiley, 1971.

Weiss, Lynn. *Attention Deficit Disorder in Adults.* Dallas: Taylor Publishing, 1992.

Whalen, C. K., *et al.* "A Social Ecology of Hyperactive Boys: Medication Effects in Structured Classroom Environments." *Journal Appl Behav Anal,* 12 (1979), 65-81.

Wilson, John. *Thomas Carlyle: The Iconoclast of Modern Shams.* 1973.

Winn, Marie. *The Plug-In Drug.* New York: Bantam, 1978.

Wolkenberg, F. "Out of a Darkness." *The New York Times Magazine,* October 11, 1987.

Recommended reading:

- *Focus your Energy: Hunting for Success in Business with Attention Deficit Disorder.* Thom Hartmann. Pocket Books, 1994

- *ADD Success Stories: A Guide to Fulfillment for Families with Attention Deficit Disorder.* Thom Hartmann, Underwood Books, September, 1995.

- *Women with Attention Deficit Disorder: Embracing Disorganization at Home and in the Workplace.* Sari Solden, Underwood Books, October, 1995.

- *Driven To Distraction.* Edward Hallowell, MD, and John Ratey, M.D. Pantheon Press, 1994.

- *How to Raise a Healthy Child ... In Spite of Your Doctor.* Robert S. Mendelsohn, M.D. Contemporary Books, 1984.

- *Attention Deficit Disorder in Adults: Practical Help for Sufferers and their Spouses.* Lynn Weiss. Taylor Publishing, 1992.

- *You Mean I'm not Lazy, Stupid or Crazy?!* Kate Kelley and Peggy Remundo. Scribners, 1995

• *Beyond ADD: Hunting For Reasons In the Past & Present*. Thom Hartmann. Underwood Books, 1996.

• *The Prophet's Way: Touching the Power of Life*. Thom Hartmann. Mythical Books, 1997.

Index